WATERGATE
and the Resignation of President Nixon

By Christine Honders

Portions of this book originally appeared in
Watergate by Michael V. Uschan.

LUCENT
P R E S S

Published in 2019 by
Lucent Press, an Imprint of Greenhaven Publishing, LLC
353 3rd Avenue
Suite 255
New York, NY 10010

Designer: Deanna Paternostro
Editor: Jessica Moore

Library of Congress Cataloging-in-Publication Data

Names: Honders, Christine, author.
Title: Watergate and the resignation of President Nixon / Christine Honders.
Description: New York : Lucent Press, 2019. | Series: American history |
  Includes bibliographical references and index.
Identifiers: LCCN 2018002900 (print) | LCCN 2018001497 (ebook) | ISBN
  9781534564282 (eBook) | ISBN 9781534564275 (library bound book) | ISBN
  9781534564299 (pbk. book)
Subjects: LCSH: Watergate Affair, 1972-1974--Juvenile literature. | Nixon,
  Richard M. (Richard Milhous), 1913-1994--Resignation from office--Juvenile
  literature. | United States--Politics and government--1969-1974--Juvenile
  literature.
Classification: LCC E860 (print) | LCC E860 .H66 2019 (ebook) | DDC
  973.924092--dc23
LC record available at https://lccn.loc.gov/2018002900

Printed in the United States of America

CPSIA compliance information: Batch #BS18KL: For further information contact Greenhaven Publishing LLC, New York, New York at
1-844-317-7404.

Please visit our website, www.greenhavenpublishing.com. For a free color catalog of all our high-quality books, call toll free 1-844-317-7404 or fax 1-844-317-7405.

Contents

Foreword   4

Setting the Scene: A Timeline   6

Introduction:
The End of American Innocence   8

Chapter One:
"One of Us"   12

Chapter Two:
A Third-Rate Burglary   29

Chapter Three:
Investigation and Cover-Up   46

Chapter Four:
Taking Down a Presidency   57

Chapter Five:
The Nixon Tapes   68

Epilogue:
The Watergate Effect   80

Notes   92

For More Information   98

Index   100

Picture Credits   103

About the Author   104

Foreword

The United States is a relatively young country. It has existed as its own nation for more than 200 years, but compared to nations such as China that have existed since ancient times, it is still in its infancy. However, the United States has grown and accomplished much since its birth in 1776. What started as a loose confederation of former British colonies has grown into a major world power whose influence is felt around the globe.

How did the United States manage to develop into a global superpower in such a short time? The answer lies in a close study of its unique history. The story of America is unlike any other—filled with colorful characters, a variety of exciting settings, and events too incredible to be anything other than true.

Too often, the experience of history is lost among the basic facts: names, dates, places, laws, treaties, and battles. These fill countless textbooks, but they are rarely compelling on their own. Far more interesting are the stories that surround those

basic facts. It is in discovering those stories that students are able to see history as a subject filled with life—and a subject that says as much about the present as it does about the past.

The titles in this series allow readers to immerse themselves in the action at pivotal historical moments. They also encourage readers to discuss complex issues in American history—many of which still affect Americans today. These include racism, states' rights, civil liberties, and many other topics that are in the news today but have their roots in the earliest days of America. As such, readers are encouraged to think critically about history and current events.

Each title is filled with excellent tools for research and analysis. Fully cited quotations from historical figures, letters, speeches, and documents provide students with firsthand accounts of major events. Primary sources bring authority to the text, as well. Sidebars highlight these quotes and primary sources, as well as interesting figures and events. Annotated bibliographies allow students to locate and evaluate sources for further information on the subject.

A deep understanding of America's past is necessary to understand its present and its future. Sometimes you have to look back in order to see how to best move forward, and that is certainly true when writing the next chapter in the American story.

1946
Richard Nixon wins
a seat in Congress,
defeating Jerry Voorhis.

1952
On September 23, Nixon
defends himself against
charges of improper
campaign spending with his
"Checkers" speech and
is elected vice president
in November.

1960
Nixon loses the
presidential race to
John F. Kennedy.

1946	1948	1952	1960	1963	1965

1963
President Kennedy
is assassinated.

1965
The first U.S. combat
troops see action in
the Vietnam War.

1948
Nixon brings accused Russian
spy Alger Hiss to the House
Un-American Activities
Committee, bringing Nixon
into the national spotlight.

A Timeline

1974
Nixon hands over transcripts of recorded conversations subpoenaed by the Watergate special prosecutor. Three articles of impeachment are brought against the president, and he resigns from the presidency.

1969
On January 20, Nixon is inaugurated as the 37th President of the United States.

1969	1971	1972	1973	1974

1971
On February 16, Nixon begins secretly recording conversations in the Oval Office and Cabinet Room of the White House.

1972
Nixon is reelected in a landslide victory.

1973
The U.S. Senate creates a committee to investigate Nixon's campaign activities. Nixon, John Dean III, and H. R. Haldeman discuss Watergate and the cover-up. Alexander Butterfield tells the Senate committee that there is a secret recording system in the White House.

THE END OF AMERICAN INNOCENCE

In 1972, the arrest of five men burglarizing an office of the Democratic National Committee (DNC) in the Watergate Hotel changed the American political climate forever. The crime did not seem that intriguing until it was revealed that the men involved had possible ties to President Richard Nixon. This arrest became one small link in a much more complex chain of events that introduced the public to the lengths some people will go to remain in power.

The hotel burglary led investigators down a path of political corruption that the public had never seen before. Secret activities in the White House were revealed, and it was revealed that money was illegally diverted to fund these activities. People were hired to disrupt the 1972 presidential campaign and sabotage George S. McGovern, the Democratic nominee. Eventually, it was discovered that the president probably not only

knew about these activities, but went to great lengths to cover them up.

In 1974, Congress voted to begin impeachment proceedings against President Nixon. Nixon, with evidence piling up against him, resigned from the presidency in August 1974 to avoid facing impeachment.

Before Watergate, the public trusted politicians to uphold the U.S. Constitution and to hold the interests of the American people above their own. Since then, public mistrust of politics has grown along with the demand for more scrutiny of government officials and policies. Even today, the name "Watergate" is automatically associated with corruption and scandal, and the disillusionment that started with the Watergate scandal still haunts American politics.

A Pattern of Misconduct

Until June 1972, few people outside of

Washington, D.C., had heard of Watergate, a complex of six buildings which housed a fashionable hotel, offices, apartments, and a retail center with stores and restaurants. That changed after five men—Bernard L. Barker, Virgilio R. Gonzalez, Eugenio R. Martinez, Frank A. Sturgis, and James W. McCord Jr.—were arrested in the early hours of June 17 for breaking into the office of the DNC.

At first, the incident barely made headlines, but it picked up speed across the nation and around the world as hundreds of stories in newspapers and on television began linking the break-in to President Richard Nixon's campaign. Nixon, a Republican, was running for a second term against Democratic Senator George S. McGovern of South Dakota.

News reports said that the men who were arrested were working for the Committee to Re-elect the President (CRP), a fundraising organization created by Nixon. Their mission had been to steal

On the 45th anniversary of the Watergate scandal in 2017, room 214, the hotel room where the break-in was planned, was renamed the "Scandal Room." Guests could pay $800 a night to stay in the 1970s-themed room in the complex shown here.

information on how the Democrats were planning to defeat Nixon. The failed burglary became even more important when investigators learned that McCord was a security chief for the CRP and that two coconspirators who were arrested later—G. Gordon Liddy and E. Howard Hunt Jr.—had ties to Nixon. Liddy had been working as a counsel for the CRP and Hunt had recently been hired as a staff member in the White House.

Former U.S. attorney general John Mitchell headed the CRP. Fearful that a full investigation of the incident would doom Nixon's chances to be reelected, the day after the burglary, Mitchell and Jeb Magruder, his top assistant, decided that the best way to handle it was to conceal the involvement of the White House.

The cover-up eventually involved not only Mitchell and other top campaign officials, but also members of Nixon's White House staff and the president himself. This illegal effort included destroying evidence; lying to law enforcement officials, judges, and members of Congress; and attempts to force the Federal Bureau of Investigation (FBI) to halt their investigation into the incident. According to author Fred Emery in his book, *Watergate: The Corruption of American Politics and the Fall of Richard Nixon*, it was the cover-up, not the break-in, that forced Nixon to resign. Emery wrote, "It was a pattern of malfeasance [misconduct] by him [Nixon] and his men that led to [Nixon having to leave office]."[1]

The Power of the Press

The White House cover-up continued for nearly two years. It failed in part because two *Washington Post* newspaper reporters refused to stop investigating the burglary. Carl Bernstein and Bob Woodward stayed with the story for many months to uncover how White House officials had illegally tried to conceal White House participation in Watergate. They also turned up evidence that the Nixon administration had, in the past, illegally monitored telephone conversations of private citizens and government officials for political purposes. They also discovered that the White House had authorized another burglary in 1971 to gain the medical records of a government worker who had leaked secret papers on the Vietnam War to a newspaper.

Bernstein and Woodward, however, were only catalysts who ignited the government's actions. Their reporting and growing public anger over the effort to cover up the political scandal that became known as Watergate led a Senate committee in May 1973 to formally investigate the burglary. In nationally televised hearings, the Senate Watergate Committee questioned top White House staff members and gained access to transcripts and tape recordings of talks between the president and his staff concerning Watergate. The Senate investigation led to new revelations about what happened, including details on Nixon's involvement in the cover-up.

The committee unearthed so much

damaging information about Nixon that the House Judiciary Committee began proceedings on July 27, 1974, to impeach him for obstructing justice.

Less than two weeks later, on August 8, 1974, Nixon resigned as president. He believed that resigning would be less disgraceful than being tried, found guilty, and thrown out of office by Congress. The day after resigning, Nixon left the nation's capital, and Vice President Gerald R. Ford was sworn in as president.

The Watergate Effect

Watergate had a major impact on the political climate. People were not just disappointed in the dishonesty of their president—they now had evidence of bad behavior by their politicians. As a result, it is not uncommon for Americans to assume that many of their politicians engage in dishonest or unethical behavior.

Government representatives who once worked in obscurity are now hounded by the media. Some believe that this is because of the demand for transparency by public officials. Others believe that it is a result of the public's appetite for stories about lies and inappropriate behavior. Either way, the divide between the media and American politicians has continued to deepen in the decades following Watergate.

Watergate changed American politics and American opinions about politicians in a monumental way, and it did so without the kind of violence that often accompanies this kind of massive national shift in perspective. Author Thomas Mallon, who was alive during Watergate, said, "People talk of Watergate as a moment when America lost its innocence, and there's probably something to that. But the entire thing happened without a soldier in the street, without a gun being fired. It showed the sophistication of American law and life."[2]

Chapter One

"ONE OF US"

Nixon's first campaign slogan when he ran for Congress was "One of Us." Richard Nixon did not come from a wealthy family. He was raised in a traditional, small town in southern California. His father was a grocer, and his mother was often absent. He lost two of his brothers at a young age. He was a hard worker and was serious and awkward as a boy, once writing his mother when he was 10, saying, "I wish you would come home right now." He signed the letter, "Your good dog, Richard."[3] As a child, Nixon listened to faraway train whistles and said he wished could go out into the world to make a difference.

It was his difficult childhood that made the boy develop into the man that he eventually became. His poverty made him a target of other kids' teasing. Even as an adult, he felt snubbed by the "elite" crowd, whom he began to resent, or feel bitter toward. Nixon had learned to be mistrustful of others, and others were mistrustful of him.

It was this paranoia that led him to his downfall as president. He recorded his phone conversations and meetings. He was obsessed with leaks to the press. He directed an almost hatred toward those he perceived to be his enemies.

However, there was another side to Richard Nixon. According to his friends, he was intelligent and kind. His presidential agenda was very progressive for the Republican Party at the time, championing health care reform, civil rights for women and minorities, and environmental protections. He worked to establish a relationship with China, and he improved U.S. relations with the Soviet Union.

Richard Nixon was fierce, driven, and hardworking. He wanted the best for the American people, yet he allowed suspicion and paranoia to influence his decisions. Watergate exposed Nixon as a human being with many flaws. He was indeed "one of us."

Early Life

Richard Milhous Nixon was born on January 9, 1913, in Yorba Linda, California. Richard's parents, Francis (Frank) A. Nixon and Hannah Milhous Nixon, were Quakers, which heavily influenced their son. In 1922, the family's 12-acre (9 ha) lemon grove failed, so the family moved to Whittier, California, where Frank started a combination grocery store and gas station.

Richard, his four brothers, and his mother all worked in the family business. When Nixon was in high school, he woke up daily at 4 a.m. and drove to nearby Los Angeles, California, to buy fresh vegetables. He washed them and set them out for customers at his father's grocery store before going to school. Nixon learned valuable lessons from his father. "He left me a respect for learning and hard work; and the will to keep fighting no matter what,"[4] Nixon wrote as an adult.

Despite their hard work, the Nixons were poor. "We had very little," Nixon claimed. "I wore my brother's shoes, and my brother below me wore mine. We never ate out—never. We certainly had to learn the value of money."[5] During the Great Depression that began in 1929, many families were struggling. Nixon, however, felt humiliated because of his hand-me-down clothes, and he resented people who looked down on him because of his poverty. He also had difficulty making friends because he was shy, which made him feel like an outsider. According to Nixon, his childhood experiences made him determined to show people who snubbed him that he could be successful. In a 1974 interview, Nixon explained,

What starts the process, really, are laughs, slights and snubs when you are a kid. Sometimes it's because you're poor, or Irish or Jewish or Catholic or ugly or simply that you are skinny. But if you are reasonably intelligent and if your anger is deep enough and strong enough, you learn you can change those attitudes by excellence [and] personal gut performance.[6]

Nixon channeled his inner anger into becoming a top student. He attended Whittier College in his hometown with hopes of becoming rich and famous.

The Haves and Have-Nots

Nixon attended Whittier College on a scholarship started by his wealthy maternal grandfather for family members. His scholarship made Nixon feel like a second-class student compared to the wealthier students. His feeling of being an outsider was heightened when the Franklins, a literary and social club at Whittier, rejected his membership application. Bitter about the rejection, Nixon then started a club he named

Richard Nixon was the second of five children. He played violin in the high school orchestra.

On October 29, 1929, the stock market collapsed, causing a financial crisis. In a short time, the unemployment rate grew to 25 percent, and wages dropped by nearly 50 percent. Shown here are people waiting for a meal in a Depression-era bread line.

the Orthogonians; the name was made up. Nixon once said of the two groups, "They [the Franklins] were the haves and we were the have-nots."[7]

Nixon was determined to prove to the Franklins he was as good as they were. He studied furiously and honed his speaking skills on the debate team.

He also won an election for president of the student body by promising to eliminate a ban on student dances. Ola-Florence Welch, his college girlfriend, claimed that Nixon was unhappy. She said, "He seemed lonely, and so solemn at school. He didn't know how to mix. He was smart and sort of set apart. I think he was unsure of himself, deep down."[8]

Nixon finished second in his 1934 graduating class and won a scholarship to Duke Law School in Durham, North Carolina. Nixon worked in the school library for spending money, which again made him feel inferior to the other students. Even though Nixon was not popular, he was elected president of his law school bar association in 1936 because students respected his intellectual achievements.

An Onstage Romance

In 1937, Nixon graduated third in his class at Duke Law School. Nixon had dreamed of working for a big New York law firm, but he failed to get such a high-paying position. He was also rejected by the FBI when he applied for a job as an agent. Feeling defeated, Nixon returned to Whittier to work for Wingert and Bewley, a small, local law firm.

A year later, Nixon auditioned for and won a part as a college student in *The Dark Tower*, a murder mystery play being produced by a local theater group. Some Nixon biographers believe he did this to meet prospective clients and show his involvement in community affairs. During the play, Nixon met Thelma Catherine Ryan, who would become his wife. Ryan was a teacher known to friends as "Pat," because she was born on March 16, hours before St. Patrick's Day. They began dating and were married in a Quaker ceremony on June 21, 1940, in Riverside, California.

Unethical Attacks

Nixon was not content being a small-town lawyer. In 1941, he was offered a position in Washington, D.C., with the new Office of Price Administration, a federal agency created by President Franklin D. Roosevelt to regulate the pricing of consumer goods and impose rationing programs. World War II was being waged in Europe, and many products were scarce and expensive. Nixon jumped at the chance to leave Whittier for new opportunities in Washington, D.C.

Shortly before Nixon was to move to Washington, D.C., on December 7, 1941, Japan bombed Pearl Harbor in Hawai'i, and the United States entered World War II. Nixon chose to fight for his country, and in April 1942, he joined the U.S. Navy, even though his Quaker faith opposed military service. "It was a difficult decision for me to make," Nixon admitted, "but I felt that I could not sit back while my country was being attacked."[9] Nixon served as a ground operations officer, supervising movements of supplies and men from island to island as U.S. forces advanced through the Pacific.

When Nixon was discharged from service in 1946, he decided to run for Congress in California as a Republican in the 1946 election. His opponent was Democrat Jerry Voorhis, who had held the seat since 1937. The election was dominated by the Cold War, a period

Pat Nixon was the earliest first lady to support the Equal Rights Amendment. She also announced publicly that she supported a woman's right to choose to have an abortion following the Roe v. Wade *Supreme Court decision in 1973.*

Nixon established him as a loyal anti-Communist legislator, which was exactly the kind of person most Americans wanted to elect during the Cold War.

of political hostility from 1947 to 1991 between the Communist Soviet Union and its associated states and the United States and its democratic allies.

Nixon took advantage of the American public's anti-Communist feelings at the time to defeat Voorhis. He claimed Voorhis had favored the Soviet Union through votes in Congress and believed he was a Communist sympathizer. Voorhis actually opposed Communism, and historians say Nixon falsified claims against the Democrat to win. Years later, even Nixon admitted his attacks had been unethical. He said, "Of course, I know Jerry Voorhis wasn't a Communist … I suppose there was scarcely ever a man with higher ideals than Jerry Voorhis, or better motivated … But … I had to win. That's the thing you don't understand. The important thing is to win."[10]

Dirty Tactics

Nixon continued his anti-Communist crusade in Congress as a member of the House Un-American Activities Committee (HUAC). The committee held hearings to identify Communist spies or sympathizers in the United States. On August 3, 1948, Whittaker Chambers, a former Communist Party member, claimed Alger Hiss was a Communist. Hiss was a former State Department official who had helped establish the United Nations.

Two days later, Hiss testified before the committee that he had never been a Communist or met Chambers.

Nixon, however, believed Hiss had been evasive in his testimony and was lying. Nixon said, "I saw that he had never once said flatly, 'I don't know Whittaker Chambers.'"[11] At Nixon's request, the HUAC kept questioning Hiss until he finally admitted he had known Chambers. Hiss was found guilty of perjury for lying to the committee and sentenced to five years in prison.

Nixon's exposure of Hiss made him a hero in the fight against Communism, and in 1950, he used that notoriety to run for a vacant U.S. Senate seat. His opponent was Democrat Helen Gahagan Douglas, another California U.S. representative. Although Douglas opposed Communism, she had once voted against funding for the HUAC because she did not feel Communism was a threat to the United States. Nixon claimed that because of that vote, Douglas was a Communist sympathizer.

Nixon also made other false claims about Douglas being a Communist. Because the color red was associated with Communism, Nixon nicknamed Douglas the "pink lady" and sent out 500,000 fliers on pink paper "with vague but ominous suggestions that Helen Douglas had secret Communist ties … Nixon campaign staffers would call voters at home and ask if they knew that Helen Douglas 'was married to a Jew' and suggest that she was just another 'movie Jew' trying to take the country away from 'real' Americans."[12]

Alger Hiss, accused of spying for the Soviet Union, went to prison for denying under oath that he gave government secrets to a key Communist Party member. He died in 1996, still insisting he was innocent.

A California newspaper was so upset at Nixon's campaign tactics that they labeled Nixon "Tricky Dick," a nickname that he carried the rest of his life. However, Nixon's dirty political tactics worked, and he won the Senate race.

Second in Command

Nixon once told a friend that he ran for the Senate because "the House offered too slow a road to leadership, and I went for broke."[13] It did not take long for Nixon to take another big step politically. In the summer of 1952, presidential candidate Dwight D. Eisenhower, the U.S. Army general who helped win World War II, chose Nixon as his running mate because of his strong anti-Communist credentials.

After being nominated, however, Nixon was hit with allegations that

A Campaign Contribution

On September 23, 1952, Nixon appeared on television to defend himself against charges that he had illegally used campaign funds to pay for personal expenses. He listed his family's financial status to the public in an almost embarrassingly honest way, even saying that his wife did not have a fur coat like many Democrats' wives, instead she had a "respectable Republican cloth coat." The most memorable part of the speech was when he talked about the one political gift he accepted, the family dog, Checkers:

> We did get something, a gift, after the election.
>
> A man down in Texas heard Pat on the radio mention the fact that our two youngsters would like to have a dog, and, believe it or not, the day before we left on this campaign trip we got a message from Union Station in Baltimore, saying they had a package for us. We went down to get it. You know what it was?
>
> It was a little cocker spaniel dog, in a crate that he [the man] had sent all the way from Texas, black and white, spotted, and our little girl Tricia, the six year old, named it Checkers.
>
> And you know, the kids, like all kids, loved the dog, and I just want to say this, right now, that regardless of what they say about it, we are going to keep it.[1]

The speech redeemed Nixon, and Eisenhower and Nixon won the 1952 presidential election.

1. Richard M. Nixon, "Checkers Speech," The History Place Great Speeches Collection, accessed on February 2, 2018. www.historyplace.com/speeches/nixon-checkers.htm.

he was illegally paying his personal expenses with campaign funds. Fearing that Eisenhower would drop him, on September 23, 1952, Nixon made the bold move of defending himself in a televised speech. It is legal for politicians to use campaign contributions for political purposes, such as travel expenses, and Nixon told viewers that "every penny of it [campaign contributions] was used to pay for political expenses that I did not think

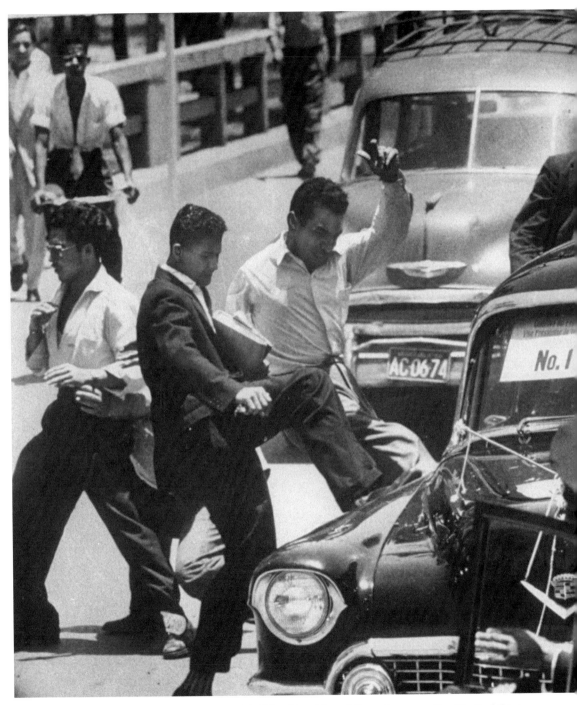

Citizens of Latin America were upset with Vice President Nixon because the United States was backing dictatorial regimes in the region rather than helping the people directly by providing them with economic assistance. Some are shown here attacking Nixon's car.

should be charged to the taxpayers of the United States."[14]

Although his critics claimed Nixon did not answer the allegations that he used campaign funds for personal expenses, he won over the public with his speech. Eisenhower kept him as his running mate, and on November 4, they won the election.

For two terms— from 1953 to 1961—Nixon was a strong, active vice president who enhanced the power and prestige of a position that had previously been unimportant. This was partly because Nixon was the first vice president required to temporarily run the government after Eisenhower became incapacitated by medical problems. Nixon briefly took over the duties of president when Eisenhower had a heart attack on September 24, 1955; a bout with ileitis (an intestinal infection) in June 1956; and a stroke on November 25, 1957.

Nixon was also highly visible to the entire world during a half-dozen trips he made to Europe, Latin America, and the Middle East to gain the support of foreign countries for U.S. policies. Nixon showed strong leadership skills on May 9, 1958, when he remained calm after anti-American protesters threw rocks at his limousine and threatened his life when he visited Caracas, Venezuela. On July 24, 1959, he claimed democracy was

The First Televised Debates

Television in 1960 was still a relatively new medium, but it was growing in power and influence. In his book, *The Making of the President 1960*, historian Theodore H. White claimed—as do many other historians—that the first debate between John F. Kennedy and Richard M. Nixon on September 29, 1960, was key to Kennedy's victory. White wrote that both candidates spoke intelligently about their plans for the future but that Kennedy was more appealing to viewers because of his youthful, energetic appearance. White described how the candidates looked on television:

> *Kennedy was calm and nerveless in appearance. The vice president, by contrast, was tense, almost frightened, at turns glowering and, occasionally, haggard-looking to the point of sickness. [Nixon] has a broad, almost sunny smile when he is with friends. His is a broad open face and the deep eye wells, the heavy brows, the broad forehead give it a clean, masculine quality. Yet on television, the deep eye wells and the heavy brows cast shadows on the face and his eyes glowered on the screen darkly; when he became rhetorically indignant, the television showed ferocity; when he turned, his apparently thin brush of hair showed in u glimmering widow's peak.*[1]

1. Theodore H. White, *The Making of the President 1960*. New York, NY: Atheneum, 1961, p. 186.

superior to communism in a spirited debate with Soviet leader Nikita Khrushchev in Moscow, Russia. It was called the Kitchen Debate because it took place in a kitchen that was part of a U.S. exhibit at the American National Exhibition. Many Americans considered Nixon heroic by having an unplanned discussion with the Soviet leader.

Eisenhower also appreciated Nixon's work as vice president. He once wrote to Nixon: "You have brought to the office of Vice President a real stature that formerly it had not known."[15] Nixon gained so much experience that he believed he deserved to be the next president, and in 1960, he ran against Democratic nominee John F. Kennedy.

Nixon's opponent in the 1960 presidential race, John F. Kennedy (right), was a young, unknown senator from Massachusetts. Historians believe that if it was not for that first televised debate, Kennedy may never have become president.

The Near End of a Political Career

Nixon was the favorite in the 1960 presidential election because many people believed his service as vice president made him more qualified than Kennedy to be president. However, Kennedy was attractive, charismatic, a hero of World War II, and an eloquent speaker, and those factors made him a formidable candidate.

On September 26, 1960, Nixon and Kennedy met for the first of four televised debates. Both candidates effectively defended their positions on issues, but Kennedy appeared handsome, strong, and confident while Nixon seemed nervous and looked tired because he had been sick for two weeks with a knee infection. A national poll the next day showed 43 percent of viewers believed Kennedy had won the debate while 23 percent thought Nixon had won.

The election was one of the closest in history at the time, and Kennedy won by only 114,673 votes out of more than 68 million cast. Many people thought Nixon should have challenged the balloting in Illinois and Texas because of widespread reports of improper voting. Nixon, in fact, could have won if those votes had gone to him—4,500 in Illinois and 28,000 in Texas, giving him the electoral votes he needed to win the presidency. Nixon reportedly wanted to file a challenge but listened to advice from Eisenhower, who told him not to because it would create intense political division that could weaken the country. The loss left Nixon bitter. It also made him more willing to do anything to win an election. "I vowed," Nixon said, "that I would never again enter an election at a disadvantage by being vulnerable to them [his opponents]—or anyone—on the level of political tactics."[16]

Nixon returned to California where he practiced law and wrote *Six Crises*, a book about his long career in politics. The book became a best seller, boosting his fame and leading Republicans to ask him to run for governor of California in 1962 against Governor Pat Brown. When Nixon lost by 300,000 votes, most people believed his political career was over. Nixon seemed to confirm that the night of his defeat in an angry tirade against newspaper reporters, who he blamed for his defeat because of negative stories they wrote about his candidacy. He bitterly told reporters, "You won't have Nixon to kick around anymore, because, gentlemen, this is my last press conference."[17]

Winning It All

Nixon moved to New York and became a partner in a prestigious law firm. Despite his vow to quit politics, Nixon campaigned heavily for Arizona senator Barry Goldwater in the 1964 presidential election when he unsuccessfully ran against Democratic president Lyndon B. Johnson. Nixon's efforts raised his stature with Republicans so much that, in 1968, he decided to run again for president.

To improve his image as a bitter loser, Nixon tried to recast himself as the "New Nixon," someone who was more open and understanding of the problems of average Americans. Historian Theodore H. White wrote, "the snarl and self-pity … were gone … [and what Nixon was showing now] was genuine and authentic, true to the inner man."[18] He tried to connect with the public by appearing on the hit television comedy *Laugh-In*, where he said humorous catchphrases from the show that had become popular with viewers.

The Vietnam War, which had divided the nation, was the main issue in the 1968 presidential election. Johnson became so unpopular for sending hundreds of thousands of American troops

President Lyndon B. Johnson (second from right) and wife "Lady Bird" Johnson (far right) are shown here with Nixon and his family before Nixon's 1969 inauguration.

to fight in the war that on March 31, 1968, he announced he would not run for reelection. Vice President Hubert H. Humphrey won the Democratic nomination, and Alabama governor George Wallace was the presidential candidate for the new American Independent Party, one of the strongest independent parties in U.S. history.

Nixon believed the United States should continue fighting and win the conflict in Vietnam. To win supporters, Nixon said he could bring the war to an end quickly and honorably with North Vietnam, hinting at a "secret plan." Nixon, however, later said he never had a specific strategy for achieving peace. In his memoirs, he wrote, "I never said that I had a 'plan,' much less a 'secret plan,' to end the war. I was deliberately straightforward about the difficulty of finding a solution. As I told the AP [Associated Press] on March 14, 1968, there was 'no magic formula, no gimmick [to end it].'"[19]

However, many voters were led to believe that Nixon had a secret plan to end the war. This, and his promises to crack down on illegal drugs and end the military service draft, helped him win the election.

The Harder the Fall

The rise of Richard Nixon reads like a classic American success story: a shy, awkward man works his way up from poverty into public service to finally win the highest political seat in America. However, he achieved that position by using dishonest or unethical campaign tactics in an effort to defeat his enemies. In the end, he became a victim in his own game. During his last speech in the East Room of the White House in 1974, Nixon said, "Always remember others may hate you ... but those who hate you don't win unless you hate them and then you destroy yourself."[20]

Chapter Two

A THIRD-RATE BURGLARY

More than four decades after Watergate, the main question about it is still unanswered: Why?

Why did the president of the United States go so far to guarantee reelection in a race that he was already winning? Part of the answer lies in Richard Nixon's personality. He was fixated on his enemies, and even before the Watergate break-in, there are several recordings of Nixon suggesting to his staff that they burglarize opponents' offices to get information to use for blackmail (the act of threatening another person with revealing secret information unless they give money or do what someone else wants). When activist Daniel Ellsberg released secret government documents, known as the Pentagon Papers, about Vietnam to the press in 1971, Nixon was furious. He was known to rant and rave about the media, liberals, and anti-war protesters

using derogatory and prejudiced slurs, screaming about how they were all out to get him.

Nixon also was fixated on Democratic senator Ted Kennedy. Although Kennedy was not seeking the presidency in 1972, Nixon knew he would be influential in the campaign. Former White House chief of staff to Nixon, H. R. Haldeman, wrote in his book, *The Haldeman Diaries*, that Nixon said, "I'd really like to get Kennedy taped."[21]

Haldeman also said that Nixon talked about photographing Kennedy in compromising situations and leaking the photos to the press.

What most historians believe is that Watergate never would have happened without Vietnam. Although Nixon campaigned to bring the war to an end, he actually reversed a decision made by President Johnson and resumed bombing in North Vietnam. He also sent troops into Cambodia and Laos. Anti-war protests became common and increasingly violent. Most infamous was a protest at Kent State University on May 4, 1970, when the Ohio National Guard fired into a crowd of unarmed protesters, killing four students and wounding nine.

Nixon viewed anti-war protesters as subversives and attempted to implement a plan to break in and search the homes of people suspected as domestic security threats. While this plan was never realized, it revealed much about Nixon and his desire to squash any potential threats to his power.

Four days after the break-in at Watergate, Nixon's press secretary gave his dismissive take on what happened, describing the

The Second Indochina War

The United States participated in the Vietnam War from 1959 until April 30, 1975, when its last soldiers left South Vietnam. The war lasted longer than any other in U.S. history at that time.

The Vietnam War is also known as the Second Indochina War. In Vietnam, it is called the American War. In the mid-19th century, France used its superior military and economic strength to make Cambodia, Laos, and Vietnam its colonies. France called the area Indochina, and it governed the region, sometimes brutally, and benefited economically from its natural resources. In the 20th century, the Vietnamese began demanding the right to rule themselves. Ho Chi Minh, a Communist, created the League for the Independence of Vietnam, which is better known as the Viet Minh. After World War II, the Viet Minh began a war with France for Vietnam's independence. After the Viet Minh triumphed in 1954, the United Nations (UN) divided Vietnam in half. North Vietnam was led by Ho Chi Minh with a Communist form of government, and South Vietnam was led by Ngo Dinh Diem with a U.S.-backed, democratic, anti-Communist government. The UN said it would hold a national election in 1956 to unify Vietnam. However, when North Vietnamese leader Ho Chi Minh began gaining popularity around the country, it was feared that his Communist party would win. The United States and South Vietnam never allowed the election to happen, leaving the country divided and opening the door for North Vietnam to begin a military campaign for control of all Vietnam. In 1959, the United States began helping South Vietnam as part of its Cold War battle against Communism around the world.

incident as a third-rate, or very poor, burglary. Two years later, Senator Sam Ervin, chairman of the Senate Watergate Committee, gave his answer. The president and his aides had "a lust for political power." That lust, he explained, "blinded them to ethical considerations and legal requirements; to Aristotle's aphorism [statement] that the good of man must be the end of politics."[22]

Vietnam Divided

In 1955, Communist North Vietnam started using military force to obtain control of South Vietnam. The United States had provided military aid in the form of weapons and funds to South Vietnam since it had been created, and by 1963, 16,000 U.S. soldiers

By 1957, a North Vietnamese-backed group called the Viet Cong began an assault of terrorism in South Vietnam. Despite U.S. training, the South Vietnamese army was no match for their guerrilla warfare tactics, which involved booby traps, mines, and kidnappings.

were in South Vietnam. During Lyndon B. Johnson's presidency, South Vietnam was losing the conflict, so he sent more soldiers over to fight. By 1969, the number of Americans fighting there totaled more than 500,000.

Many Americans grew angry that so many U.S. soldiers were being killed and wounded in a war they could not seem to win, and one that many felt the United States had no right or reason to be involved in. They also resented the draft, a law that allowed the federal government to force men to join the armed forces. People began staging anti-war demonstrations to demand that the United States withdraw from the war. Many protests became violent. Other citizens, however, supported the war, because they believed the nation needed to fight Communism. The result was political turmoil and division throughout the nation.

After Nixon was elected, he still refused to explain how he would end the war. In May 1969, he told the nation that "peace cannot be achieved overnight ... cannot be settled in a single stroke."[23] Nixon did not predict a quick resolution to the conflict, but he was determined to defeat the Communists and avoid becoming the first president to lose a war.

In 1972, Nixon reduced the number of U.S. troops in Vietnam to 69,000 to calm the nation's growing anti-war sentiment. However, even as Nixon was bringing soldiers home, he was expanding the war to neighboring Cambodia. Cambodia was officially neutral in the conflict, but on March 17, 1969, Nixon ordered bombing attacks on trails in Cambodia that the North Vietnamese were using to get supplies to their soldiers in South Vietnam. The bombings remained secret until May 9, when the *New York Times* published a story about them. The front-page story increased anti-war sentiment against Nixon. The story also made Nixon so furious that he began to use illegal tactics to fight his critics and opponents.

Stopping the Leaks

An angry Nixon told his aides, "Find out who leaked it [the bombing story], and fire him!"[24] He ordered the FBI to place wiretaps on the telephones of officials who he suspected of giving the secret information to the *New York Times* and on the telephones of journalists who may have received the information.

Nixon continued using telephone wiretaps, both legally and illegally, for the rest of his presidency to identify people who leaked news items that hurt him or to discover what his opponents were doing. This effort increased dramatically after the *New York Times* printed a top-secret government report on June 13, 1971. The report, known as the Pentagon Papers, detailed how the United States became involved in the Vietnam War and how it had slowly escalated its participation in the conflict. The report increased anti-war sentiment,

The Pentagon Papers exposed President Harry Truman, who gave aid to France during its war with Ho Chi Minh. They also revealed that President Johnson ordered the bombing of North Vietnam in 1965 against the recommendation of U.S. intelligence reports.

and a national Gallup poll soon showed that, for the first time, a majority of Americans wanted to end U.S. participation in the war.

The president had Attorney General John Mitchell file a lawsuit to stop the *New York Times* from publishing the report. Claiming that its publication threatened national security, Mitchell was able to obtain a restraining order to stop the *New York Times* from printing it. The *New York Times* then gave the documents to other newspapers for them to publish. On June 30, the U.S. Supreme Court, in a ruling that vindicated freedom of the press, allowed the report to be printed.

Nixon was furious and demanded an end to all leaks. He did not care how it was done and ordered his staff to "do whatever has to be done to stop these leaks and prevent further unauthorized disclosures." Nixon also said, "I want it done. Whatever the cost."[25] His staff created the White House Special Investigations Unit, which became known as the Plumbers because their job was to stop "leaks." Nixon aide John Ehrlichman oversaw the activities of this group, which included E. Howard Hunt and G. Gordon Liddy, who would later become central figures in the Watergate burglary.

The Plumbers learned that former Defense Department analyst Daniel Ellsberg, who now opposed the war, had given the Pentagon Papers to the *New York Times*. On July 27, the FBI reported to White House aides that Ellsberg had been treated by Lewis Fielding, a Los Angeles psychiatrist. Liddy and Hunt suggested the Plumbers break into Fielding's office to get Ellsberg's medical records, which might have information that could be used to tarnish Ellsberg's reputation. Ehrlichman discussed the suggestion with Nixon, who verbally approved it. Ehrlichman told the Plumbers to perform the burglary. However, in a written memo, he warned them it could only be "done under your assurance that it is not traceable."[26] Ehrlichman meant that they could only perform the burglary if they were certain not to leave evidence connecting the illegal act to Nixon.

The Plumbers burglarized Fielding's office on September 2, but they failed to find any negative information about Ellsberg. The burglary was similar to the one that would be repeated a year later at Watergate.

Anti-War Sentiment Increases

Nixon is credited with some successes in his first term. On September 5, 1969, the U.S. Supreme Court ordered Mississippi to immediately begin desegregating schools. The Nixon administration enforced the ruling in Mississippi and neighboring states, and by the fall of 1970, 2 million black children across the South were attending integrated schools. In foreign affairs, Nixon is hailed for his February 1972 trip to the People's Republic of China to meet Communist leader Mao Zedong. The trip opened a new era of diplomacy

President Nixon's visit to China marked the formal acknowledgement of the "One-China" principle that recognizes Taiwan as part of China.

between the two nations, who two decades earlier had fought each other in the Korean War.

Despite his accomplishments, many Americans were unhappy with Nixon because he had failed to end the Vietnam War. Nixon had gradually reduced the number of soldiers

After shooting tear gas at demonstrators at Kent State University, National Guardsmen eventually shot and killed four students and wounded nine more. It is unclear if Guardsmen were ordered to shoot or if someone shot at them first.

fighting there through his policy of Vietnamization, which required South Vietnam to take over more combat roles. Peace

negotiations with North Vietnam were proceeding very slowly. At the same time that Nixon was withdrawing troops from South Vietnam, he was also preparing to increase bombing attacks on North Vietnam and Cambodia.

On April 30, 1970, Nixon infuriated anti-war opponents again when he announced on television that U.S. troops would enter Cambodia to attack North Vietnamese sanctuaries. In his address, Nixon said, "To protect our men who are in Vietnam and to guarantee the continued success of our withdrawal and Vietnamization programs, I have concluded that the time has come for action."[27] The expansion of the war into Cambodia ignited the most violent anti-war demonstrations the United States had seen yet. Many protests took place on college campuses as students vented their anger over the war by destroying school property or rampaging through surrounding areas. Students even took control of campuses for brief periods until police arrested them. Some protests were so severe that state governments called out the National Guard to police the violence.

At Kent State University in Kent, Ohio, students broke store windows in the adjacent town and burned down a school building that housed a military training program. On May 4, the Ohio National Guard was trying to control about 2,000 student and anti-war protesters at Kent State when nervous guardsmen, fearing for their own safety, opened fire on the unarmed crowd. The shots killed four students and wounded nine more. Two of the slain students—Allison Krause and Jeffrey Miller—were protesters, but Sandra Scheuer and William Knox Schroeder were not. They were killed while walking to class.

Nixon despised the anti-war protesters for opposing his policy. He issued a statement about the Kent State tragedy that made him seem more upset by the protesters' behavior than the deaths of the students. "This," Nixon said, "should remind us all once again that when dissent turns to violence it invites tragedy."[28] The president's insensitive reaction to the deaths of the four students added to the anger of anti-war protesters, who called the shooting the "Kent State Massacre." The reaction to events at Kent State ignited a wave of violent protests at college campuses across the nation. Two more students were killed on May 14 at Jackson State College in Jackson, Mississippi, in a confrontation with local and state police.

By 1970, however, college students were not the only ones protesting the Vietnam War, and the war became the focal point of Nixon's bid to win a second term as president.

Nixon's Campaign Opponent

By 1972, many Democratic elected officials and even a few Republicans believed the United States should withdraw from the Vietnam War, because there seemed to be no way to stop North Vietnam from winning.

One of the most vocal national officials to oppose the war was U.S. senator George McGovern of South Dakota. When McGovern realized Nixon was still trying to continue the war, he was the first senator to openly criticize Nixon for failing to fulfill his promise to end the conflict. In a speech on March 17, 1969, only a few months after Nixon was sworn in as president, McGovern said, "There is no more time for considering 'military options,' no more time for 'improving the bargaining position [with North Vietnam]' … I believe the only acceptable objective now is an immediate end to the killing."[29]

In response to the Cambodian invasion, McGovern and Republican senator Mark Hatfield of Oregon introduced a bill to Congress in May 1970 to cut off funding for military operations in Cambodia and Laos, which bordered South Vietnam. The bill also required the withdrawal of all U.S. soldiers by the end of 1971. McGovern bitterly scolded his fellow senators when they rejected the measure. He claimed they had a moral responsibility for the deaths of U.S. soldiers in the war. McGovern said, "Every Senator in this chamber is partly responsible for sending 50,000 young Americans to an early grave. This chamber reeks of blood."[30]

McGovern's stature for opposing the war rose despite his failure to pass the measure. His strong anti-war credentials helped him win the 1972 Democratic nomination for president,

George McGovern is shown here at the 1972 Democratic National Convention in Florida. McGovern supported liberal issues including civil rights and anti-poverty legislation.

"Not Quite What I Had In Mind"

G. Gordon Liddy compiled an elaborate, $1 million plan of "dirty tricks" under pressure from Nixon to gain damaging information about his Democratic presidential opponent and to fight anti-war sentiments. Liddy presented the plan, called Operation Gemstone, to Attorney General John Mitchell, with one hand bandaged. He had recently burned it in a candle flame in a bizarre attempt to show his loyalty.

The plan, with sub-operations named "Diamond," "Ruby," and "Sapphire," detailed the break-in to the DNC offices and outlined some other suggestions, including:

- sending trained street fighting squads into crowds of protesters to disrupt them before camera crews arrive on the scene
- kidnapping popular civil rights leaders and anti-war protesters by drugging them and taking them "across the border"
- luring Democrats into embarrassing and compromising positions and photographing them
- electronic surveillance, including chase planes to listen to messages between airplanes carrying Democrats

Mitchell was apparently amused at some of the more outlandish proposals. He told Liddy that "Gemstone [is] not quite what I had in mind."[1] He then told Liddy to come back to him with something cheaper and a little more realistic.

1. Richard Reeves, *President Nixon: Alone in the White House*. New York, NY: Simon and Schuster, 2001, p. 430.

which meant he would face Nixon in the election.

CREEP

To raise money and manage his second bid for the presidency, Nixon created the Committee to Re-elect the President. Its initials were CRP, but many, especially his political foes, referred to it as "CREEP." The committee was headed by John Mitchell, who had resigned as attorney general to run the campaign. Despite rising anti-war sentiment, Nixon was heavily favored to beat McGovern because many Americans still supported the war. To ensure Nixon would win,

G. Gordon Liddy (center) was the only defendant in the Watergate trials who refused to give information to prosecutors. He said it was more important to him to preserve the Nixon presidency.

Mitchell set aside $250,000 in a fund devoted to finding out the Democratic Party's campaign plans.

The White House Plumbers were disbanded in the fall of 1971. However, G. Gordon Liddy and E. Howard Hunt, who had been involved in the burglary of Daniel Ellsberg's psychiatrist's office, still worked for the White House and the CRP. They proposed Operation Gemstone, a secret plan to spy on and disrupt the Democratic presidential campaign. One of their suggestions was to break into the offices of the Democratic National Committee (DNC), which was running McGovern's campaign. Liddy and Hunt wanted to place wiretaps on telephone lines and photograph documents to obtain information that would help Nixon beat McGovern. Their main target was the office of DNC chairman Lawrence O'Brien.

On March 30, 1972, Mitchell discussed the Watergate break-in with Jeb Magruder, a former presidential assistant working for CRP, and presidential assistant Frederick C. LaRue, one of many White House aides working to reelect Nixon. Mitchell expressed doubt that the break-in would work. He asked, "How do we know that these guys know what they're doing?"[31] Despite his reservations, Mitchell approved the plan that day.

In late April, Magruder met with Liddy and told him to go ahead with the burglary. "We want to know whatever's said in his office, just as if it were here, what goes on in this office," he instructed Liddy. "Get in there as soon as you can, Gordon; it's important."[32] Magruder also told Liddy to photograph campaign documents, especially lists of people who had donated money to McGovern's campaign.

Committing the Crime

Liddy and Hunt recruited a break-in team and began preparing for the illegal act on May 22, the same day Nixon arrived in Moscow for a meeting with leaders of the Soviet Union. The burglars began by visiting Watergate, a large complex of six buildings, to gather information about its physical layout. James W. McCord Jr., a former Central Intelligence Agency (CIA) agent now working for CRP, rented room 419 in the Howard Johnson Motor Inn opposite Watergate. The room served as a meeting place for the team and would be a listening post for the wiretaps. Alfred Baldwin was stationed in the room to monitor the taps. Liddy, Hunt, and four others who helped McCord in the break-in—Bernard L. Barker, Frank A. Sturgis, Eugenio R. Martinez, and Virgilio R. Gonzalez—also rented rooms in the Watergate Hotel.

The burglars tried unsuccessfully for two nights to gain access to the DNC offices. On May 26, they failed to get from the Watergate Hotel to the adjoining office building before the security system activated at 11 p.m. in the corridor connecting the two halves of the complex. The next night, they gained entry directly to the office building, but they could not open the locked doors of the DNC offices. The team finally succeeded in breaking in on May 28 and placed two telephone bugs and photographed documents. Liddy and Hunt participated in the break-in by monitoring the activities of the burglars from the Watergate Hotel via radio contact.

For the next few weeks, team members monitored conversations in the DNC offices from the Howard Johnson hotel room across the street. However, one bug was not working, and the

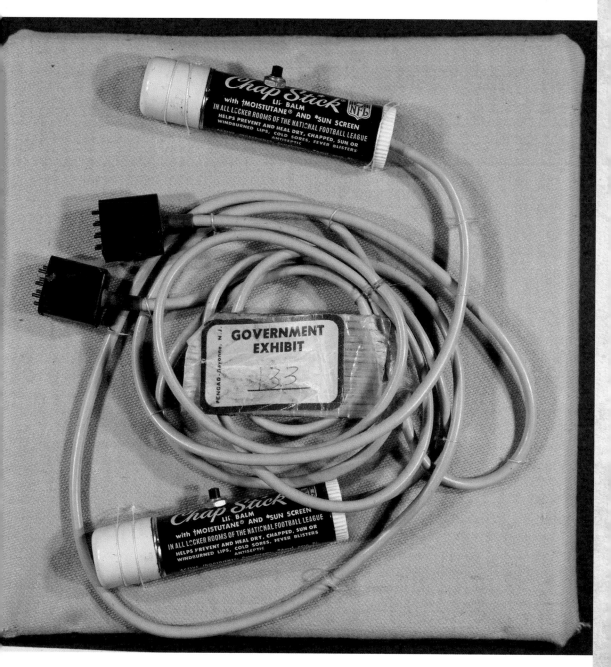

These lip balm tubes with microphones hidden inside them were found in Hunt's White House office safe. They were reportedly used by Hunt and Liddy to keep in contact with the burglars during the break-in.

second had been put in the wrong place. Magruder was unhappy with the surveillance, and on June 12, he told Liddy to send the team back to fix the problems. He also wanted more photographs of documents. "Take all the men, all the cameras you need,"[33] he told Liddy. Liddy said Magruder especially wanted data from DNC Chairman O'Brien's office.

Caught

On Saturday, June 17, 1972, Liddy and Hunt again remained in the Watergate Hotel rooms while McCord, Barker, Gonzalez, Martinez, and Sturgis broke into the DNC offices. McCord had earlier taped open the lock on a garage-level door leading to a stairwell to the DNC offices, but when the team got to that door, the tape was gone. Gonzalez, a locksmith, then opened the door and several other locked doors and taped them to stay open. The five then proceeded to the DNC offices and began their work.

While the break-in was underway, security guard Frank Wills discovered some of the taped-open doors. After asking a superior what to do, Wills called police at 1:47 a.m. to report a suspected break-in. Responding to the call were three members of a tactical unit dressed in civilian clothes—Sergeant Paul Leeper and Officers John Barrett and Carl Shoffler. The trio began a floor-by-floor search of the office building and eventually found the burglars. In his book *Watergate: The Corruption of American Politics and the Fall of Richard Nixon*, historian Fred Emery described how the burglars were arrested:

Inside the DNC the team had been moving toward its tasks: Gonzalez to open the glass door to O'Brien's suite, McCord accompanying Barker to the file area, Sturgis and Martinez were on guard at the door. McCord says he picked up some college press credential forms for the Democratic convention … [Then] Sturgis arrived saying somebody was coming. A light went on and they heard shouts of "Come out, police!" The team's exit was barred; they had no alternative but to crouch down, hoping not to be seen …

McCord has said that were the police search less thorough, they might have escaped detection. But the police searched each cubicle in the DNC in turn. Officer Barrett was the first to spot an arm move behind the glass [partition] and shouted, "Hold it. Come out." Sergeant Leeper, who had also drawn his revolver, jumped onto a desk, looked over the partition, and saw five men. They were raising their hands, which he remembered were covered with blue rubber gloves. Some were trying to remove the gloves.

At this point, Liddy says, came the first and last transmission, a whisper, from the entry team: "They got us."[34]

The three policemen were surprised by the five burglars, who did not seem like typical burglars. They were wearing business suits and rubber gloves. They also had equipment not normally found on burglars—listening devices, film and two cameras, three pen-size tear-gas guns, a walkie-talkie, and almost $2,300 in cash.

Police took them to jail and charged them with felonious burglary and possession of implements of crime—the burglary tools they used to open doors—in what at first seemed to be a bizarre, but minor burglary. Wills was hailed as a hero for discovering the break-in. "I did the right thing," said Wills. "I was just doing my job."[35]

No one that night could have predicted the outcome of Wills having done his job properly. The arrests would explode into the biggest political scandal in U.S. history and lead to the downfall of a president.

Chapter Three

INVESTIGATION AND COVER-UP

With new political scandals in the news almost daily, history may have been more forgiving to President Nixon if it were not for his actions after the burglary. He said during a press conference, "I can say categorically that … no one in the White House staff, no one in this Administration, presently employed, was involved in this very bizarre incident."[36] Nixon's press secretary Ron Ziegler referred to it as a very poor burglary attempt. Meanwhile, Magruder and other CRP members were already destroying evidence. Taped conversations would later reveal that Nixon was directly involved in the cover-up. For the first time in history, there was evidence that the president violated the trust of the American people.

Reporters may not have pursued the story so aggressively had it not been for Nixon's public disdain for the press. In 1969, in response to leaks to the press about Vietnam, his national security adviser Henry Kissinger ordered wiretaps to be placed on 17 journalists. In 1971, during a taped conversation, Nixon said, "In the short run, it would be so much easier, wouldn't it, to run this war in a dictatorial way, kill all the reporters and carry on the war."[37]

Watergate changed the course of journalism. It began with *Washington Post* reporters Carl Bernstein and Bob Woodward's interest in a story at the bottom of the front page on June 18, 1972. Other newspapers ignored the story, and the White House criticized the *Washington Post* as biased and liberal leaning. Woodward and Bernstein, however, through their relentless investigative journalism and an anonymous, high-ranking, government informant, pursued the story until there was no doubt of Nixon's involvement. Watergate sparked a new interest in investigative reporting and is still a major part of American journalism.

Destroying Evidence

When the burglars were arrested, Liddy and Hunt realized they could be traced to their hotel rooms at the Watergate. They frantically packed up electronic equipment and other incriminating evidence and quickly left. Alfred Baldwin was in the Howard Johnson room that served as a listening post for the telephone taps. He also fled with electronic equipment and other evidence that could be linked to the burglary.

Liddy went home. When his wife woke up at about 3 a.m. as he was going to bed, Liddy told her, "There was trouble. Some people got caught. I'll probably be going to jail."[38] Hunt went to his office at the White House and put the electronic equipment, an address book, and a notebook with information on his CRP activities into a safe. Hunt then called attorney Douglas Caddy and asked him to represent the men who had been arrested—James W. McCord Jr., Bernard L. Barker, Virgilio R. Gonzalez, Eugenio R. Martinez, and Frank A. Sturgis.

The burglars, meanwhile, were obstructing the investigation by giving police false identities, something they were instructed to do if arrested. McCord and Sturgis were even carrying fake identification from their time with the CIA. The attempts to mislead authorities failed because police identified them by their fingerprints.

While the five were waiting to be charged, Liddy began destroying evidence connecting the burglary to the White House. After a few hours of sleep, Liddy got up at 7 a.m. and tried to call CRP staffer Jeb Magruder. When he learned Magruder was in Los Angeles with John Mitchell, where it was only 4 a.m., he decided to talk to him about the botched burglary later. Liddy drove to the CRP offices and used a shredder to destroy Operation Gemstone documents and other evidence linking the burglary to the president's campaign. He even shredded $100 bills that were part of thousands of dollars the campaign had given him to fund Gemstone because he feared the bills could be traced to the CRP's financial records through their serial numbers. Liddy then went to the White House and called Magruder. He used a White House telephone to make the call because it was a secure line that could not be electronically tapped.

Magruder was upset. He told Mitchell that his main concern was that the burglars could be linked to the CRP. That also concerned Mitchell, who was especially worried about McCord, who worked directly for the campaign. Mitchell had an aide call Attorney General Richard Kleindienst and order him to get McCord out of jail before his identity was discovered. When Kleindienst refused, Magruder, Mitchell, and White House aide Frederick LaRue continued discussing their options in

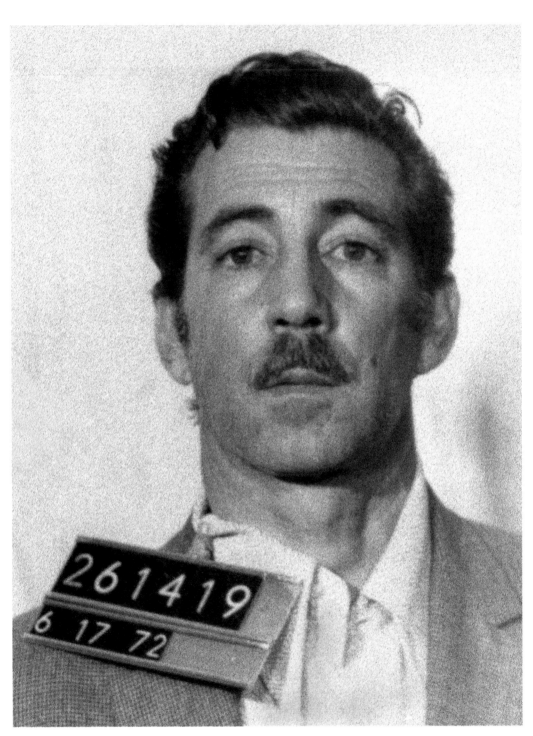

Virgilio Gonzalez was a locksmith who fled from Fidel Castro's Communist Cuba to the United States in 1959. He was later a suspect in the assassination of President Kennedy.

handling the situation. It was during this discussion that Magruder began to understand the seriousness of the situation and that they needed to protect the president. He said, "I realized that this was not just hard-nosed politics, this was a crime that could destroy us all. The cover-up, thus, was immediate and automatic; no one ever considered that there would not be a cover-up. It seemed inconceivable that with our political power we could not erase this mistake we had made."[39]

It was, however, too late to stop the incident from being made public. The burglars were already being formally charged in court with the crime they had committed.

"5 Held in Plot to Bug Democrats' Office Here"

The burglars were arraigned at 3:30 p.m. on Saturday, June 17, before Judge James A. Belsen. When Belsen asked the men their professions, one said they were dedicated to fighting Communism, and several others agreed with that description. McCord said he worked as a security consultant and had recently retired from government service. When Belsen asked "Where in government?" McCord replied softly, "CIA."[40]

McCord had tried to speak in a whisper so one else in the courtroom would hear him, but *Washington Post* reporter Bob Woodward understood the response. Realizing it was significant that a former government spy

was involved in a break-in, Woodward took a cab back to his office to make sure that information was added to the story about the burglary before the 6:30 p.m. deadline for the next day's edition of the newspaper. On Sunday, June 18, the *Washington Post* carried a front-page story on the burglary. Eight reporters, including Bob Woodward and Carl Bernstein, had contributed facts to the story. Under the headline "5 Held in Plot to Bug Democrats' Office Here," its opening paragraph read, "Five men, one of whom said he is a former employee of the Central Intelligence Agency, were arrested at 2:30 A.M. yesterday in what authorities described as an elaborate plot to bug the offices of the Democratic National Committee here."[41]

In just a few hours, the reporters had gathered key facts about the burglars, including that four were exiles from Cuba and that Sturgis had helped train Cuban exiles for the failed 1961 Bay of Pigs invasion to overthrow Communist leader Fidel Castro. Like most burglars, they had tools to pick locks. However, the story noted that unlike most burglars, they were wearing rubber gloves to conceal their fingerprints, had sophisticated electronic equipment, and carried almost $2,300 in cash, most of it in $100 bills with consecutive serial numbers. The five men were charged with felony burglary and possession of implements of crime. Bail was set at $50,000 each for 4 of them and $30,000 for McCord; his bail was lower because he lived locally and was considered less of a risk to flee the area.

The fact that McCord was a former government spy gave the incident ominous overtones. In a follow-up story later that Sunday, the Associated Press (AP) news agency reported that McCord was the security coordinator for Nixon's reelection campaign. The connection to the CRP made the burglary a much bigger story. The *Washington Post* assigned Woodward and Bernstein to continue investigating the burglary full time because of the political ramifications it now had for the upcoming presidential election.

While reporters such as Woodward and Bernstein were scrambling to uncover facts about the burglary, however, CRP and White House staff members were working to keep them buried.

Nixon Gets Involved

In California, Mitchell gave reporters a written statement about the burglary on Monday, June 19. The statement said that McCord had installed security systems for the campaign, but that the CRP had not ordered McCord to perform the burglary. It also said, "We want to emphasize that this man and the other people involved were not operating either on our behalf or with our consent. I am surprised and dismayed at these reports."[42]

Mitchell's lie about the CRP and McCord is just one example of how the president's staff were working to conceal evidence of their involvement in the burglary. Magruder destroyed

Gemstone files he had at his home. John W. Dean III, who advised Nixon on legal matters, went through the contents of Hunt's White House safe. Wearing rubber gloves to avoid leaving fingerprints, Dean removed documents concerning the burglary and other illegal activities connected to the CRP.

It is unknown exactly when or how Nixon learned that his reelection campaign had planned and carried out the burglary, but it was probably the day after it occurred. The news frightened Nixon, who feared that the FBI would discover the connection. Mitchell devised a plan to make the FBI stop probing Watergate. He wanted the White House to persuade deputy CIA director Vernon Walters to ask acting FBI director L. Patrick Gray to stop investigating Watergate. The FBI handles domestic crime and security threats to the nation, while the CIA focuses on foreign threats to the United States. The two federal agencies have a working agreement to stay out of each other's affairs when their interests overlap. Because four of the burglars were Cuban, Mitchell wanted Walters to tell Gray that the incident involved Cuba, which would make it a CIA responsibility.

Mitchell did not tell the president directly about his plan. However, on June 23, Haldeman had several conversations in the White House with Nixon about Mitchell's suggestion on how to handle the FBI. Nixon liked the plan and even added some details to

The failed invasion at the Bay of Pigs resulted in Castro taking 1,100 prisoners. After secret ransom negotiations with President Kennedy, Castro released the prisoners for $53 million in food and medicine.

make the CIA explanation to the FBI more believable. Nixon suggested that the Bay of Pigs—the failed attempt by Cuban exiles supported by the U.S. government to invade Communist Cuba in 1961—could be used as an excuse to keep the Watergate information private as a matter of national security. Nixon told Haldeman, "[Say to the CIA that] the President's belief is that this is going to open the whole Bay of Pigs thing up again … and that they [the CIA] should call the FBI in and say that we wish for the country [not to] go any further into this case."[43]

This is believed to be the first time Nixon took an active part in the cover-up of White House involvement in Watergate. Walters was contacted later that day, and he called Gray. However, stopping the FBI investigation was impossible, because the Watergate investigation was being conducted by Earl Silbert, a U.S. attorney for the District of Columbia.

The FBI, on Silbert's orders, continued investigating the burglary and the men who had committed it—so did Woodward and Bernstein, who were digging up key facts about White House involvement in Watergate.

The Investigation Begins

Although Woodward reported about McCord's CIA past in his newspaper's first Watergate story, he made the mistake of not checking out McCord's background more thoroughly. If he had, he would have learned that McCord was a CRP employee. The AP, however, did discover it, and the AP is credited with the "scoop"—being the first to report the information. Woodward redeemed himself the next day. He learned from another reporter that references to a "Mr. Howard" and a "Mr. H. H." appeared in notebooks the burglars had when they were arrested.

Woodward was able to identify the man as E. Howard Hunt. He telephoned the White House to see if Hunt worked there. He was surprised to learn that Hunt was a consultant to Charles Colson, who handled political matters for Nixon, including his campaign.

Woodward immediately called Hunt, who refused to comment. Woodward then telephoned Ken W. Clawson, a former *Washington Post* reporter who was the White House deputy director of communications. Clawson admitted that Hunt had done some security work for Colson but was no longer employed by the White House. Clawson then claimed, "[No one] at the White House had any knowledge of, or participation in, this deplorable incident at the Democratic National Committee."[44] Woodward thought the comment was suspicious because Clawson volunteered it without being asked if there was a White House connection. Woodward's next story about Watergate on June 20 described what he had learned, establishing another key link between the burglars and the White House.

Carl Bernstein discovered that a $25,000 check given to the CRP by a

This address book, found in a room of the Watergate Hotel, has an entry "HH" with a phone number labeled "WH." That number was confirmed to be the White House, and "HH" was Howard Hunt.

political donor had been deposited in Bernard L. Barker's Florida bank account, and his story about it was published August 1. CRP officials claimed they did not know how the money got into Barker's account. However, the financial connection between the CRP and Barker made more people suspect the burglary had been ordered by campaign or White House officials.

The Democrats Fight Back

From the beginning, Democrats believed the CRP and the White House were responsible for the break-in. On June 20, DNC chairman Lawrence O'Brien filed a $1 million lawsuit against the CRP for invasion of privacy

A Partnership Forms

Although many reporters investigated Watergate, Bob Woodward and Carl Bernstein are given the most credit on breaking the story. Because they shared a byline for their Watergate stories, they were nicknamed "Woodstein." Their book *All the President's Men* explained how they began to work as a team:

Gradually, Bernstein and Woodward's mutual distrust and suspicions diminished. They realized the advantage of working together, particularly because their temperaments were so dissimilar. The breadth of the story, the inherent risks and the need for caution all argued for at least two reporters working on it. By dividing the work and pooling their information, they increased their contacts ...

To those who sat nearby in the [Washington Post] newsroom, it was obvious that Woodstein was not always a smoothly operating piece of journalistic machinery. The two fought, often openly. Sometimes they battled for fifteen minutes over a word or sentence. Nuances were critically important; the emphasis had to be just right. The search for the journalistic mean was frequently conducted at full volume, and it was not uncommon to see one stalk away from the other's desk. Sooner or later, however (usually later), the story was hammered out.[1]

1. Quoted in Carl Bernstein and Bob Woodward, *All the President's Men.* New York, NY: Simon and Schuster, 1974, pp. 49–50.

and violation of the party's civil rights. O'Brien claimed the burglary had been politically motivated by the Republicans. He said, "Continuing disclosures in the wake of Saturday's bugging incident at the DNC raise the ugliest questions about the integrity of the political process that I have encountered in a quarter century of political activity."[45] O'Brien called for a full investigation of the burglary to punish those responsible for it.

Despite news stories linking the White House to Watergate, Nixon remained far ahead of Senator George McGovern in his bid for reelection. So far, the nation was not that interested in the story.

Nixon Wins a Second Term

McGovern tried to use Watergate against Nixon during the presidential campaign. He called Watergate "a moral and Constitutional crisis of unprecedented dimensions" and claimed that "the whole ugly mess of corruption, of sabotage, of wiretapping [belonged] squarely in the lap of Richard Nixon."[46] O'Brien and other well-known Democrats also tried to make voters angry about Watergate. Most Americans, however, were slow to consider it a major issue in the campaign.

On June 21, just a few days after the burglary, the president spoke with Haldeman about the effect Watergate would have on his campaign. Nixon still believed it would not hurt his reelection chances because most people would not be surprised by it. He said,

The reaction is going to be primarily [by political figures in] Washington and not the country [average citizens], because I think the country doesn't give much [concern] about it. [Most] people around the country think that this is routine, that everybody's trying to bug everybody else, it's politics. That's my view.[47]

Nixon was correct in his belief that the public would be unconcerned with Watergate in the first months after the burglary. Nixon retained his substantial lead over McGovern in election polls despite a continuing flow of damaging stories suggesting Watergate's connection to his campaign staff.

It is likely that Nixon would have lost the election if voters had known he was concealing the truth. Instead, they elected him to a second term. In fact, Nixon defeated McGovern in one of the largest landslides in U.S. political history. Nixon won 60.7 percent of the votes and captured every state except Massachusetts and Washington, D.C. Minor outrage over the Watergate scandal and Nixon's failure to end the Vietnam War, however, resulted in more Democrats being elected to Congress, where they already held substantial majorities in both the House and Senate.

A Hollow Victory

Although it seems impossible with the political climate surrounding Watergate, Nixon easily won the election, taking 97 percent of the electoral votes. The Vietnam War, which was still raging on, had a significant impact on the election. The Democratic nominee George McGovern was vocally anti-war and vowed to get U.S. troops home within 90 days. This was still too radical a position for most Americans, who believed that total withdrawal would be the end of South Vietnam. Nixon's strategy in Vietnam and the recent boost in the American economy are what likely won

Nixon and Vice President Spiro Agnew's (right) crushing victory over McGovern was a turning point for the Republican Party, which had suffered a similar defeat when Johnson defeated Republican candidate Barry Goldwater in a landslide in 1964.

him the election.

Nixon wrote in his memoir that his happiness in winning his second term was overshadowed by concern over Watergate. He also expressed sadness over not having ended the Vietnam War and believed that those factors cost him dearly in losing control of Congress. He had no idea at the time how much more Watergate was going to cost him.

Chapter Four

TAKING DOWN A PRESIDENCY

On the surface, it seemed that President Nixon was at the height of his political career. He had just won reelection in one of the largest landslides in history. Earlier in 1972, he was the first president to travel to China to have dinner with Chinese Premier Zhou Enlai in Beijing, extending diplomacy to the Far East. After more negotiations with North Vietnam, in January 1973, an agreement was reached and signed in Paris that included a cease-fire, withdrawal of American troops, and the release of all prisoners of war.

Watergate loomed in the background. The first Watergate trial was set to begin just two weeks before Nixon's inauguration. The trial focused on the burglary, and the White House continued to treat it as a non-story. However, the presiding judge wanted more information about the White House's possible involvement. He was determined to find out if there was a broader conspiracy. Enough evidence was established during that trial for the Senate to vote unanimously to form a special committee to investigate possible abuses during Nixon's campaign. The third-rate burglary was about to blow the doors of the White House wide open.

Guilty

The first Watergate trial began on January 8, 1973, before federal judge John Sirica. Neither the defendants nor Nixon were happy that Sirica was the judge. He was a tough judge who had been nicknamed "Maximum John" because he often gave criminals the maximum sentences the law allowed.

Liddy, Hunt, McCord, Barker, Gonzalez, Martinez, and Sturgis were charged with conspiracy, burglary, and wiretapping. In a pretrial hearing, Sirica said his goal was to find out all the facts of the burglary, including why it was done and who ordered and financed it.

Hunt, Barker, Gonzalez, Martinez, and Sturgis all pled guilty, and Liddy and McCord went to trial. As the trial progressed, Sirica did not think prosecuting attorneys were questioning the defendants thoroughly enough about the break-in, so Sirica asked his own questions.

Sirica wanted to know where the burglars got the thousands of dollars in $100 bills they had when they were arrested. The fact that the serial numbers on the bills were consecutively numbered was suspicious because it showed that the bills had come from the same source. When the judge asked Barker how he got his money, Barker said he had received the $100 bills by mail in a blank envelope. Knowing Barker was not answering truthfully, Sirica bluntly responded, "I'm sorry. I don't believe you."[48]

Jurors heard testimony from 60 witnesses and viewed more than 100 pieces of evidence. On January 30, jurors took less than 90 minutes to decide McCord and Liddy were guilty. Sirica set sentencing for March for all seven men. Despite the guilty verdicts, Sirica was unhappy the trial had failed to uncover more details about a crime with serious political overtones. Sirica told the defendants, "I am still not satisfied that the pertinent facts that might be available—I say might be available—have been produced before an American jury."[49] Sirica also said he hoped future investigations would discover the truth about questions the trial had failed to answer.

Peace in Southeast Asia

For four years, Nixon had tried to win the Vietnam conflict while giving in to the demands of the American public to withdraw soldiers from the unpopular war. There were 534,000 U.S. soldiers in Vietnam when Nixon became president in January 1969. However, Nixon's program of Vietnamization reduced the number of U.S. soldiers to fewer than 160,000 by 1971 and to about 23,000 by the end of 1972. He countered those troop reductions with increased aerial bombing of combat areas and North Vietnam. However, without massive numbers of U.S. soldiers on the ground, South Vietnam was losing.

Historians believe Nixon could have ended the war before the 1972 election. They claim he did not because it would have hurt his chances for reelection by appearing to give in to demands by Senator George McGovern, his Democratic opponent, to end the war. After he was reelected, Nixon urged Henry Kissinger, his foreign affairs adviser who was negotiating with North Vietnam, to accept whatever terms the Communists wanted to end the fighting. "The war weariness has reached the point that it is just too much for us to carry on,"[50] Nixon told Kissinger of public opposition to the conflict. Kissinger returned to negotiations and quickly hammered out an agreement to end the war.

On the night of January 23, 1973, Nixon went on television to announce the war was over. "I have asked for this radio and television time tonight," Nixon said, "for the purpose of announcing that we today have concluded an agreement to end the war and bring peace with honor in Vietnam and Southeast Asia."[51] Nixon told war-weary Americans that a ceasefire would go into effect on January 27, and that the remaining 23,700 U.S. soldiers would come home within 60 days. In return, North Vietnam agreed to release 651 prisoners of war.

Nixon never got much credit for ending the Vietnam War because it took him more than four years to do it. He had been elected in 1968 partly because voters believed he had a plan to quickly end the conflict, and many people now criticized

Nixon is shown here in January 1973 announcing to the nation that North and South Vietnam had reached a tentative peace agreement. Nixon promised South Vietnam's president that the United States would retaliate if the North violated the agreement. This promise was not fulfilled, however, and fighting in Vietnam continued until North Vietnam took over the South Vietnamese capital of Saigon in April 1975.

him for allowing it to continue as long as he did. In 11 years of fighting, 58,200 U.S. soldiers were killed in the Vietnam War, including almost 21,000 during his presidency. Nixon claimed he had achieved an honorable end to the war, but it was still the first one the United States did not win.

Even after the war ended, Nixon still faced many problems that continued to undermine confidence in his presidency. One of them involved criminal behavior by Vice President Spiro T. Agnew.

"The Worst of Both Worlds"

In 1968, Nixon chose Spiro T. Agnew, the governor of Maryland, as his running mate. As vice president, Agnew became valuable to Nixon for his wittiness and his ability to cleverly attack the news media and other critics of the president. However, in 1973, the U.S. Attorney's Office in Baltimore, Maryland, began investigating Agnew for political misconduct. In October, officials charged Agnew with having accepted bribes totaling more than $100,000 while serving as a Baltimore county executive, Maryland governor, and vice president. The criminal charges were devastating for the Nixon administration, which was already straining under the weight of Watergate. Alexander Haig, a former army general, became Nixon's chief of staff in 1973. When Haig heard about Agnew, he thought to himself, "God! We've got the worst of both worlds: a president who is on an impeachment trail, and a vice president who is guilty of felonies."[52]

On October 10, 1973, Agnew agreed to resign as vice president. It was part of a deal with prosecutors in which he only had to plead no contest to a single charge that he failed to report $29,500 in income received in 1967. In a no-contest plea, a defendant does not admit guilt but does not try to prove their innocence. Agnew was the second vice president to resign from office and the first to resign because of criminal charges. Two days later, Nixon named Representative Gerald R. Ford as his new vice president.

Nixon also struggled with a sinking economy that suffered from unemployment and inflation. When Nixon resigned in 1974, unemployment and inflation were both higher than when he took office. Inflation skyrocketed in 1973 partly because of a shocking increase in the price of gasoline, which rose rapidly from a national average of 38.5 cents per gallon in May 1973 to 55.1 cents in June 1974.

The reason for the giant hike was the decision on October 15, 1973, by Arab nations to limit oil production. The high gasoline prices hurt the U.S. economy, and the limited production also caused severe gasoline shortages. In some areas around the country, drivers had to wait in long lines to fill their tanks, and some stations ran out of gas. Arab nations had cut oil production to punish the United States because it backed Israel by sending them weapons during the Arab-Israeli War in 1973. While Nixon,

People found ways to adapt during the gasoline shortage that began in 1973. For example, this gas station only allowed cars to get gas on even-numbered days if their license plate ended in an even number.

through Henry Kissinger, was able to broker a peace agreement between Israel and Egypt in January 1974, the conflict did nothing to improve U.S. relations with the Arab world.

McCord's Letter

Although more reporters became interested in Watergate, *Washington Post* reporters Bob Woodward and Carl Bernstein kept coming up with the biggest scoops. Woodward had a source he called "Deep Throat" who worked in the federal government and was leaking information to him. Although his identity remained secret for many years, it was revealed in 2005 that William Mark Felt Sr., deputy director of the FBI, was Deep Throat, and he leaked information to Woodward because he believed the public deserved to know what the Nixon administration was doing.

On January 25, 1973, Felt gave Woodward one of his most important leads.

James McCord (shown here) suggested in a letter to Sirica that John Mitchell and White House aide John W. Dean III were the ones putting the pressure on him to lie under oath and that there were more people involved.

"Colson and Mitchell were behind the Watergate operation," Felt told him. "Everyone in the FBI is convinced, including Gray."[53] Felt was referring to White House aide Charles Colson; John N. Mitchell, the former attorney general and head of the CRP; and acting FBI director L. Patrick Gray. Being able to report that Colson and Mitchell directed the break-in was a major story because of their close association with the president.

One of the most important breaks in uncovering Watergate came not from reporters but from one of the burglars. On March 20, 1974, McCord delivered a letter to Sirica, who was scheduled to sentence him and the other Watergate burglars three days later. In the letter, McCord admitted he and others had lied during the trial and failed to identify other people connected to the burglary. He even explained the reason they did that. He wrote, "There was political pressure applied to the defendants to plead guilty and remain silent."[54] The letter was dated March 19, Sirica's birthday, and he told an aide, "This is the best … birthday present I've ever gotten … This is going to break the case wide open."[55]

McCord hoped Sirica would give him a lighter sentence if he cooperated with the investigation. On March 23, Sirica issued preliminary sentences for everyone but McCord that ranged between 20 and 40 years in prison. Sirica then told the burglars he would reduce their sentences if they cooperated with government prosecutors investigating the burglary. On March 28, McCord told federal prosecutors that Liddy had told him the Watergate operation had been approved by Mitchell while he was still attorney general. In November, Sirica rewarded McCord by giving him a sentence of only one to five years.

For the first time, one of the burglars connected Watergate to one of Nixon's cabinet members and closest friends. The fallout from that testimony led to more evidence that the president's staff abused their power during the campaign.

The Cover-Up Grows

An important meeting occurred on March 21, 1973, between Nixon and White House aides John W. Dean III and H. R. Haldeman. Dean had been overseeing the cover-up of Watergate, and he told Nixon the cover-up itself had become as potentially harmful to his presidency as the burglary. Dean said, "I think that … there's no doubt about the seriousness of the problem we've got. We have a cancer—within—close to the Presidency, that's growing. It's growing daily. It's compounding, it grows geometrically now, because it compounds itself."[56]

The cover-up was growing. Nixon aides bribed the burglars to remain silent about what really happened. Payments to the men involved in the burglary for trial costs and living expenses began soon after they were arrested, and between them, they received more than $400,000 during the first 8 months after the break-in. Nixon knew about the payments from the beginning. On August 1, 1972, Haldeman told Nixon that the

A Million-Dollar Deal

President Nixon knew about and approved of the bribes offered to the burglars. In a White House conversation on March 21, 1973, Nixon told John W. Dean III he could get $1 million to continue paying the men, which probably would have involved illegal cash contributions from Nixon's campaign donors. The following exchange between Dean and the president took place after Dean told Nixon that he needed more money and Nixon inquired as to how much:

DEAN: *I would say these people are going to cost, uh, a million dollars over the next, uh, two years.*

PRESIDENT NIXON: *We could get that … If you need the money … you could get the money … What I mean is, you could, you could get a million dollars. And you could get it in cash. I, I know where it could be gotten … I mean it's not easy, but it could be done.*[1]

---

1. Quoted in Stanley I. Kutler, ed., *Abuse of Power: The New Nixon Tapes*. New York, NY: Simon and Schuster, 1997, p. 254.

---

burglars had been released from jail and had been "taken care of." When Nixon asked if that had cost a lot, Haldeman told him, "It's very expensive," to which the president replied, "Well … they have to be paid. That's all there is to that. They have to be paid."[57]

As the January 1973 trial approached, Nixon aides became even more worried that the burglars would reveal the truth. On January 6, two days before the trial began, Dean telephoned Liddy. He promised to pay the men involved in the burglary to be silent about their connection to the White House if they were convicted and sent to prison so they would have money for their families. Liddy said Dean told him, "Gordon, I want to assure you; everyone's going to be taken care of—everyone."[58] Dean promised Liddy $30,000 a year and a pardon within two years for any crimes for which he was convicted.

The other men were also offered various sums of money. After the legal proceedings against them were over, they demanded more money for their silence. On March 21, Nixon and Haldeman discussed the need for more money for bribes. Nixon told Haldeman he was willing to spend another $1 million to continue buying the silence of the 7 men.

However, the day before Nixon discussed the bribes with Haldeman, McCord gave his letter to Sirica saying he was willing to testify truthfully about what happened. On March 28, McCord began revealing details about the connection between Watergate and the Nixon administration.

Dean Comes Clean

In his March 21 meeting with Nixon, Dean admitted he was worried that he and other White House aides could be charged in connection with the cover-up if it became public. When Dean learned soon afterward that McCord was going to testify, he became more frightened that he was in serious trouble for helping direct the cover-up, including bribing the burglars.

A few days after the March 21 meeting, Haldeman told Dean that the president wanted him to write a report summarizing everything that had happened involving Watergate. However, he asked Dean to lie in the report and say that neither the president nor his top aides knew about Watergate. Dean believed Nixon wanted him to write the report so that, if the truth was ever revealed, he could claim Dean masterminded the burglary and cover-up and then lied

about it to protect himself. After thinking it over for several days, Dean decided not to write the report. Several years later, Dean wrote,

> [My] thoughts finally headed down the path I knew I had to explore. The path of telling the truth if I was called upon to testify. Whatever else happened in the days, weeks and months ahead, I was not going to lie for anybody, even the President. Despite what I'd done for him, I would not take that step.[59]

Dean began meeting with federal prosecutors in early April. When Nixon learned that Dean was cooperating with officials, he knew he was in serious trouble. Nixon decided he had to show the public that he was doing something to clean up the Watergate mess.

On the evening of April 30, Nixon went on television in his first major speech about Watergate. Nixon claimed he had known nothing about the burglary and possible cover-up until March, when he learned that some of the allegations concerning his staff might be true. The president said he then ordered a new investigation into the matter to find out what had happened. "I was determined that we should get to the bottom of the matter, and that the truth should be fully brought out no matter who was involved,"[60] Nixon told the nation.

The president then announced the resignations of presidential aides Dean, Haldeman, and Ehrlichman and

John Dean was tasked with writing a report summarizing Watergate; however, he later decided not to write it because he wanted to focus on telling the truth instead.

Attorney General Richard Kleindienst. The president was trying to protect himself by denying he knew about Watergate and getting rid of people close to him who were involved in it. Kleindienst had not been involved in the cover-up but was forced to leave because Nixon claimed the FBI, which was under his jurisdiction, was not doing a good job investigating Watergate. However, Nixon never said any of the four had done anything wrong, and he even praised Haldeman and Ehrlichman as fine government officials.

The Biggest Obstacle

Dean decided to testify under oath that Nixon was involved in the cover-up from the beginning whether or not he received immunity from prosecution. He told investigators Nixon knew about the bribes. He also told them that Nixon would write out orders regarding Watergate on the daily news summaries the staff received. Those orders often instructed Haldeman on how to counter-attack the press. He also said that Nixon gave Dean orders to participate in the cover-up directly.

When Nixon found out Dean was going to cooperate with prosecutors, he tried to force him to resign. When Dean refused, Nixon told him never to reveal the activities of his administration. According to a *Washington Post* article, four White House sources called Dean "the biggest obstacle the President will have to overcome if he is to demonstrate his innocence in the Watergate cover-up."[61]

Chapter Five

THE NIXON TAPES

As convincing as Dean was during the Watergate trial, he had no solid evidence or documentation to back up his story. Everything he said was based on recollections of conversations he had with President Nixon.

In July 1973, a revelation was made by former White House aide Alexander P. Butterfield while testifying in the Watergate trial that tape recordings of meetings in the Oval Office had been regularly recorded beginning in February 1971. Nixon also had recording devices in the White House Cabinet Room, his executive office, and four of his telephones. Most people were not aware they were being taped.

Butterfield described the complex recording system to be truthful throughout his testimony, however, he was reluctant to discuss it. "It is very obvious that this could be—I cannot say that any longer—is embarrassing to our government," Butterfield said of his reluctance to say more. "And also because I felt it could be something the President would like to present at a later time in defense of his own position."[62]

In the end, it was Nixon's paranoia and mistrust that was his undoing. There was no better evidence of a cover-up than the president's own voice on recordings he made himself.

On February 7, 1973, the Senate voted 77–0 to create the Senate Select Committee on Presidential Campaign Activities to investigate political crimes that occurred during the 1972 campaign. It became known as the Senate Watergate Committee. Four Democrats—Sam J. Ervin of North Carolina, Daniel K. Inouye of Hawai'i, Joseph M. Montoya of New Mexico, and Herman E. Talmadge of Georgia—and three Republicans—Howard H. Baker Jr. of

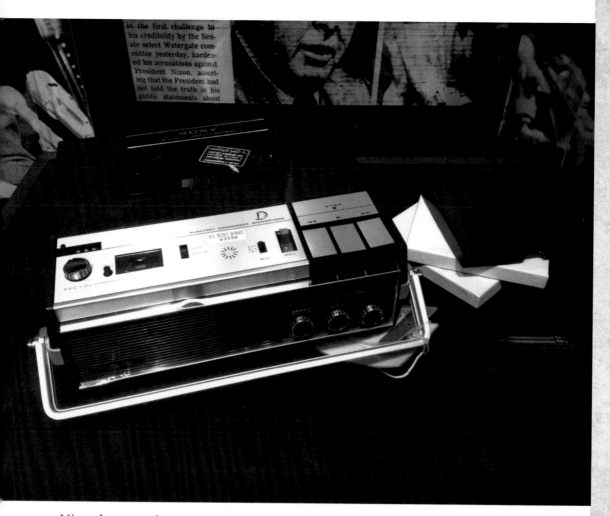

Nixon began taping conversations in 1971. Shown here is a tape recorder from his office. From February 1971 to July 1973, more than 2,600 hours of conversation were recorded.

Tennessee, Edward J. Gurney of Florida, and Lowell P. Weicker Jr. of Connecticut—were the members of the committee.

Ervin was chosen to chair the committee. Ervin was a Constitutionalist and had made comments in the past about Nixon's overreaching presidential power during the Vietnam War. Ervin's folksy mannerisms and speech belied the intelligence and ability that had made him a successful senator for two decades. During Ervin's opening statement at the first Watergate hearing on May 17, 1973, he said,

If the many allegations made to this date are true, then the burglars who broke into the headquarters of the Democratic National Committee at

The Impeachment Process

The U.S. Constitution gives Congress the power to remove a president from office through a process called impeachment. The Constitution authorizes the U.S. House of Representatives to impeach the president by charging the president with specific charges, each of which is called an "article of impeachment." If the House votes to impeach a president, the Constitution then gives the Senate the power to try the president on the articles of impeachment. At least two-thirds of senators must vote for conviction on the articles of impeachment to remove the president from office. President Richard M. Nixon resigned on August 8, 1974, before the House could impeach him. The House has impeached two presidents—Andrew Johnson in 1868 and Bill Clinton in 1998—but the Senate failed to convict either of them.

the Watergate were in effect breaking into the home of every citizen of the United States ... And if these allegations prove to be true, what they were seeking to steal was not the jewels, money or other precious property of American citizens, but something much more valuable— their most precious heritage: the right to vote in a free election.[63]

The power of Ervin's words was magnified by the fact that the hearing was broadcast live on national television. The day after that first hearing, Attorney General-designate Elliot L. Richardson launched a separate investigation into the Watergate incident. Richardson named former government attorney Archibald Cox as the Justice Department's special Watergate prosecutor. Nixon named Richardson attorney general after Richard Kleindienst resigned on April 30. Cox said his investigation was important because it could restore the public's faith in its ability to elect public officials. "Somehow," Cox said, "we must restore confidence, honor and integrity in government."[64] As a special prosecutor, Cox would have more freedom to investigate the Watergate burglary than someone who worked for the Justice Department, which was controlled by the president.

Cox and the Senate were investigating Watergate even after the burglars had been convicted, because there were still so many unanswered questions. These official probes elevated

Watergate from a minor burglary to headline news.

The Televised Trials

The Watergate hearings were some of the most sensational and widely watched programs ever televised. During the next few months, 319 hours of hearings were shown, and an estimated 85 percent of all U.S. households watched at least part of them. The hearings were also broadcast on radio stations. Millions of people turned on the hearings instead of their favorite shows because they felt they were watching history being made. There was also a morbid fascination for viewers in seeing witnesses squirm while answering tough questions. On the first day of the hearings, Ronald Coleman, a graduate of the Catholic University of America in Washington, D.C., summed up why the hearings were entertaining to watch: "We've all got a little sadistic streak in us—like stopping on the highway to watch an accident."[65]

Details began to emerge about other illegal White House activities. On June 13, the committee released a memorandum addressed to Ehrlichman that described the plan to burglarize the office of Daniel Ellsberg's psychiatrist. The news of White House involvement in the crime shook the public to its core.

The star witness of the hearings was Dean. In testimony that began on May 25, Dean explained how he and other presidential aides covered up Watergate. Some of Dean's most damaging testimony came when he described a meeting he had with Nixon on September 15, 1972. Dean testified that after the talk, he believed Nixon knew about the attempted cover-up. Dean said, "I left with the impression that the President was well aware of what had been going on regarding the success of keeping the White House out of the Watergate scandal and I also had expressed to him my concern that I was not confident the cover-up could be maintained indefinitely."[66]

Dean's statement raised many questions about what Nixon knew about Watergate. Committee member Baker summed up what senators wanted to find out when he asked Dean, "What did the president know and when did he know it?"[67] They soon found the key to those questions from Butterfield. On July 13, the committee members asked Butterfield if there were any recording devices in Nixon's office. Butterfield responded, "I was hoping you fellows wouldn't ask me that."[68] He then explained that Nixon had been taping telephone calls and meetings in the Oval Office for years.

Senate staff members were surprised. Very few people knew about the system, and they were only asking Butterfield questions in a general way, not thinking they were about to get the "smoking gun," (conclusive evidence). However, Cox and the committee realized immediately that the tapes were a key source of information about

Nixon's role in Watergate. On July 23, Cox asked Nixon for tapes from the days Dean and other witnesses claimed they had spoken with him about Watergate based on their testimony. They were met with refusal. This touched off a bitter fight for possession of the tapes that would ultimately decide Nixon's future.

Obstruction of Justice

When Nixon learned that investigators knew about the tapes, he ordered the White House recording system disconnected. Nixon knew how much damaging information was on the tapes and fought to keep them secret. Nixon refused to give the tapes to investigators, but Cox and Ervin persuaded Sirica to issue a subpoena, which is a written court order that would force Nixon to release them or face obstruction of justice charges. On July 25, Nixon again refused to surrender the tapes. In a letter to Sirica, Nixon claimed he did not have to honor the subpoena because he was the president. Nixon wrote, "The independence of the three branches of our government is at the very heart of our constitutional system. It would be [wrong] for the President to seek to compel some particular action by the courts. It is equally [wrong] for the courts to seek to compel some particular action from the President."[69]

Nixon based his refusal on executive privilege, a legal theory that claims the Constitution guarantees presidents should be free of control by the courts or Congress in carrying out their essential duties. Cox and Ervin appealed Nixon's refusal, and it would take several months for the federal court system to decide a verdict. The Senate Watergate Committee, meanwhile, had recessed its hearings in early August. Nixon used the break to claim he had not done anything wrong. "Not only was I unaware of any cover-up but … I was unaware of anything to cover up,"[70] Nixon said in an August 15 television speech.

Nixon was losing his credibility with the American people. In addition to continuing revelations about his involvement in Watergate, federal investigators were also uncovering evidence that Nixon's 1972 presidential campaign had accepted millions of dollars in illegal contributions. The allegations further tainted Nixon's reputation, and many people believed he was fighting the court order to conceal his guilt.

On October 12, 1973, a federal appeals court upheld Cox's right to the tapes. Nixon then made another attempt to conceal incriminating evidence. Nixon offered to have Republican senator John C. Stennis, a political ally, review and summarize the conversations in writing. When Cox refused that compromise, Nixon decided to have him fired.

The Saturday Night Massacre

On Saturday, October 20, Nixon ordered Attorney General Elliot

Richardson to fire Archibald Cox. Richardson refused because he believed it was wrong for a president to use his power to interfere in a criminal investigation involving himself. "A government of the laws was on the verge of becoming a government of one man,"[71] Richardson said. Richardson resigned rather than fire Cox. Nixon then asked Deputy Attorney General William Ruckelshaus to fire Cox. When Ruckelshaus also refused, Nixon fired him. Nixon finally persuaded Solicitor General Robert Bork to fire Cox. The president also abolished the office of special prosecutor and turned the investigation over to the Justice Department so that he could better control it.

Nixon's maneuver to evade criminal prosecution backfired. The news media nicknamed the series of events the Saturday Night Massacre. Newspaper and magazine editorials condemned Nixon for his actions, with many of them calling for his resignation, and news reports created a wave of public outrage against the president. The growing backlash forced him to reverse what he had done. Nixon reinstated the Special Prosecutor's Office and on November 1, named Leon Jaworski to replace Cox. The president also agreed to give transcripts of some of the subpoenaed tapes to Watergate investigators.

However, when investigators received the transcripts in mid-November, they discovered that a tape of conversations from June 20, 1972, had an unexplained 18-and-a-half-minute gap.

The missing audio was critical to the investigation because Haldeman had testified that he and Nixon discussed Watergate that day. The White House claimed Rose Mary Woods, Nixon's secretary, had accidentally erased the segment while transcribing the tape. Investigators and the public, however, believed the tape had been erased on purpose.

On November 17, Nixon defended himself in a speech to newspaper editors in Orlando, Florida. Nixon's defense was summed up by two sentences: "People have got to know whether or not their President is a crook. Well, I'm not a crook."[72]

"Contempt Equals Impeachment"

In December, Nixon declared he would not surrender any more tapes, and on January 24, 1974, he refused a request from the Senate committee for documents concerning Watergate. Nixon again claimed executive privilege, telling the senators that "to produce the material you now seek would unquestionably destroy any vestige of confidentiality of Presidential communications, thereby irreparably impairing the constitutional functions of the Office of the Presidency."[73]

The fight for the tapes was renewed on April 16 when Jaworski and the House Judiciary Committee issued subpoenas for 64 tapes. The judiciary committee had begun investigating Watergate in December to see if there was

During an hour-long press conference in 1973, Nixon said he should have monitored his campaign staff's activities more closely and that the tapes would prove that he had no involvement in the cover-up of Watergate.

The release of the transcripts meant the release of the most private information any president had ever given to the public. What they revealed about Nixon's involvement in blackmail and cover-ups shocked even his biggest supporters.

enough evidence to impeach Nixon. Because of its power to impeach Nixon, the judiciary committee's investigation now became more important than that of the Senate Watergate Committee. The committee, which was nearly finished with its investigation, gave its evidence to the House Judiciary Committee and cooperated with its probe of the president.

Nixon at first refused to surrender the tapes. One especially damaging conversation he wanted to cover up occurred on March 21, 1973, when Nixon and Dean discussed bribing the convicted burglars. On March 22, 1974, a depressed Nixon wrote in his diary, "Lowest day. Contempt equals impeachment."[74] On April 30, 1974, Nixon released 1,200 pages of heavily edited transcripts of the tapes to avoid being charged with contempt of Congress, an offense that warranted impeachment.

Jaworski and the committee rejected the transcripts and demanded the tapes. When Sirica ruled that Nixon had to release them, Nixon appealed the order to the U.S. Supreme Court. Nixon's action increased demands by elected officials, the news media, and citizens that he resign or be impeached.

On July 24, 1974, the Supreme Court, in a unanimous 8–0 decision, upheld the right of investigators to hear the tapes (the court has nine members, but Justice William Rehnquist declined to vote because he had been appointed by Nixon). The ruling, read by Chief Justice Warren Burger, said a president could not use executive privilege to withhold evidence in criminal proceedings. Nixon had to release the tapes, which included recordings of conversations that proved he had known about and helped direct the cover-up of Watergate.

The Impeachment Inquiry Begins

Three days later, the judiciary committee began formal televised hearings on whether to impeach the president. The first hearing opened with statements from committee members on why the hearings were important. No one was more impressive than Representative Barbara Jordan, a Texas Democrat. According to Jordan, the Constitution demands that Congress remove any president who has committed illegal acts. She said,

Has the President committed

offenses, and planned, and directed, and acquiesced in a course of conduct which the Constitution will not tolerate? That's the question. We know that. We know the question. We should now forthwith proceed to answer the question. It is reason, and not passion, which must guide our deliberations, guide our debate, and guide our decision.[75]

For several months before the hearings started, the judiciary committee had considered documents, tapes, and testimony gathered by the Senate Watergate Committee, special prosecutors, and its own staff. It did not take the committee long to decide whether Nixon should be impeached. On July 27, the committee voted 27–11 to approve the first article of impeachment, which charged Nixon with obstruction of justice for using his office to try to stop or hamper Watergate investigations. In the next few days, the committee approved two other articles of impeachment against Nixon: abuse of his power for political purposes by violating the rights of citizens with wiretaps and burglaries and contempt of Congress for refusing to honor its subpoenas for evidence.

Six Republicans joined the Democratic majority in voting to impeach Nixon. Republican representative Caldwell Butler of Virginia explained why he voted to impeach Nixon: "The pattern of misrepresentation and half-truths that emerges from our investigation

In the Interest of the Nation

In a televised speech the night of August 8, 1974, President Nixon told Americans he was resigning because it was the best thing for the nation. Nixon said,

> *Throughout the long and difficult period of Watergate, I have felt it was my duty to persevere, to make every possible effort to complete the term of office to which you elected me.*

> *In the past few days, however, it has become evident to me that I no longer have a strong enough political base in the Congress to justify continuing that effort. As long as there was such a base, I felt strongly that it was necessary to see the constitutional process through to its conclusion ...*

> *But with the disappearance of that base, I now believe that the constitutional purpose has been served, and there is no longer a need for the process to be prolonged.*

> *I would have preferred to carry through to the finish whatever the personal agony it would have involved, and my family unanimously urged me to do so. But the interest of the Nation must always come before any personal considerations ...*

> *I have never been a quitter. To leave office before my term is completed is abhorrent to every instinct in my body. But as President, I must put the interest of America first.*[1]

1. Richard M. Nixon, "President Nixon's Resignation Speech," PBS, August 8, 1974. www.pbs.org/newshour/spc/character/links/nixon_speech.html.

reveals a presidential policy cynically based on the premise that truth itself is negotiable."[76]

The committee recommended to the House of Representatives that Nixon be impeached on all three charges. The House then scheduled an impeachment vote for August 19. If the House, as expected, voted to impeach Nixon, the U.S. Senate would try him on the charges. If Nixon was found guilty, he would be removed from office.

Stepping Down

Many members of Congress had said they would not vote to impeach Nixon unless there was a "smoking gun." When the White House finally released the tapes on August 5, 1974, Nixon realized that his June 20, 1972, conversation with Haldeman was the smoking gun that would likely mean his impeachment. After the July 27 Supreme Court decision, Nixon realized that the full story of his involvement in the cover-up would be made public if he was impeached. Nixon began to consider resigning to avoid the embarrassment of going through such a humiliating procedure. However, he delayed a final decision on resigning until he learned what action Congress would take.

On August 7, Nixon met with three Republican congressional leaders—Senators Barry Goldwater of Arizona and Hugh Scott of Pennsylvania and Representative John Rhodes of Arizona. "Mr. President," Goldwater said,

Nixon announced that he would resign as the 37th President of the United States at noon on August 9, 1974. Vice President Gerald Ford would be sworn in as the new president.

"this isn't pleasant, but you want to know the situation and it isn't good."[77] Rhodes told Nixon the House would vote to impeach him, and Goldwater and Scott said they and other senators would vote to find him guilty in the Senate impeachment trial.

The news made Nixon realize he had to resign before he was impeached. He met later with Alexander Haig and press secretary Ron Ziegler to tell them his decision. Nixon said, "Well, I screwed it up real good, didn't I?"[78] Nixon told Ziegler to schedule a televised speech for the next evening so he could announce his resignation to the nation. On August 8, 1974, Nixon met during the day with his cabinet and other staff members to tell them he was resigning. One of his most important meetings was with Vice President Gerald Ford, who under the Constitution would become president when Nixon resigned. "Jerry, I know you'll do a good job,"[79] Nixon told him.

That night, Nixon told a television audience of 150 million people that he was resigning. Nixon mentioned Watergate but did not admit any guilt. He claimed he was stepping down because his loss of support in Congress and among U.S. citizens had weakened his ability to effectively govern the nation. Nixon did admit that his presidency had created great political divisions. Nixon said, "By taking this action I hope that I will have hastened the start of the process of healing which is so desperately needed in America."[80]

Nixon announced that his resignation would be effective at noon on August 9.

THE WATERGATE EFFECT

While Nixon prepared his resignation speech on the morning of August 8, 1974, political history was about to change. Never before had a president resigned in America, and America's view of government and the world of politics would never be the same.

In some ways, the political environment was changing for the better. Former Attorney General Elliot Richardson said, "Watergate has made one significant contribution, at least to the extent that there are many officeholders who are becoming convinced that honest politics—open, candid politics—is the best politics."[81] Congress began passing legislation on campaign finance reform and started looking into abuses of power by government agencies. The Church Committee, established in 1975 and led by Senator Frank Church, looked into accusations that the CIA, the FBI, and the National Security Agency (NSA) were illegally monitoring the activities of and spying on U.S. citizens, including Dr. Martin Luther King Jr. The reforms that the Church Committee established remain relevant today with whistleblowers such as Edward Snowden revealing just how much information the government collects on its citizens.

The field of journalism changed as well. Woodward and Bernstein wrote a book about their experience reporting on Watergate, which was adapted into a film called All the President's Men. American journalists were looked upon as aggressive, hard-hitting reporters of justice against corruption.

What Watergate changed the most was the public perception of government and politics, which seems to grow more cynical with each presidential cycle. Cover-ups and leaks are

In June 2013, former CIA systems analyst Edward Snowden leaked to the press that the NSA was secretly collecting phone communications records of millions of Americans. The NSA also tapped into the servers of internet firms to track online communication.

now part of the political vocabulary. Presidents in more recent times have become targets of suspicion rather than respected leaders. President George W. Bush was accused of leading the United States into a war with Iraq in 2003 by telling the American public that its dictator, Saddam Hussein, was producing weapons of mass destruction. Later investigations revealed that this was widely exaggerated. In 2017, Special Counsel Robert Mueller began investigating Russian interference in the 2016 presidential election, in which President Donald Trump and his staff were accused of colluding with the Russian government to sabotage Democratic nominee Hillary Clinton's campaign. Watergate was the beginning of an era in which many Americans have become numb to political scandal.

Watergate can also be looked at as

the ultimate proof of the success of the American system of government. Elizabeth Holtzman, a former representative of New York, said that Watergate was a triumph. The people realized they made a mistake when they voted Nixon in for a second term and within the following year were rallying behind Congress and the press to remove him, in "an affirmation of our system of checks and balances, working together in a historic high point in our relationship with our government."[82]

The End of the National Nightmare

At 12:03 p.m. on August 9, 1974, Gerald R. Ford took the oath of office as president in the White House East Room. Technically, he had been president since 11:35 a.m. when Nixon's resignation was delivered to the secretary of state. Ford became the 38th president and the first to take office under the 25th Amendment, which empowers the vice president to succeed the president if he dies, resigns, or is removed from office. The 25th Amendment was proposed and ratified in 1967 after the 1963 assassination of President John F. Kennedy. Ford was also the first president who had not been elected either president or vice president.

Ford said, "I assume the Presidency under extraordinary circumstances never before experienced by Americans. This is an hour of history that troubles our minds and hurts our hearts."[83] Although he did not refer directly to

Watergate or Nixon's departure in disgrace, Ford claimed, "My fellow Americans, our long national nightmare is over."[84]

However, the anguish Americans had experienced over Watergate for two years was not over because officials were still trying participants for their crimes. In fact, Americans were still wondering if the former president would be prosecuted. The likelihood that Nixon could face some sort of prosecution seemed to increase on August 20, when the House of Representatives voted 412–3 to accept the House Judiciary Committee report recommending his impeachment. Although Nixon's resignation had made impeachment unnecessary, the vote was an indication of how many members of Congress believed he was guilty.

It was now up to special Watergate prosecutor Leon Jaworski to determine if Nixon should be brought to trial. Jaworski solicited recommendations on what to do from staff members who had investigated Watergate. In a memorandum to Jaworski, attorney George Frampton wrote, "I fear that history may yet judge this venture [the investigation] a failure should your decision be to 'call it a day' and not indict former President Nixon."[85] Frampton noted, however, that public sentiment was that Nixon had suffered enough by having to resign. He also questioned whether Nixon could get a fair trial. Many people believed a fair trial was impossible because prospective jurors, having been exposed to news media coverage about Watergate, had probably already made up their minds about his guilt or innocence.

Nixon was worried that Jaworski's decision could be influenced by demands from the news media that he be charged. "They won't be satisfied until they have me in jail,"[86] Nixon told his former aides. However, Nixon's fate was soon taken out of Jaworski's hands by President Ford.

Forgiveness

When Nixon resigned, some questioned whether he had struck a deal with Ford. Nixon would resign so Ford could become president, and Ford would pardon Nixon so he would not have to stand trial for Watergate crimes. The theory seemed believable, especially after the public had learned about a meeting on August 1 between Haig and Ford. Haig met with the vice president to alert him that Nixon was considering resigning and Ford had to prepare to assume the presidency. In that meeting, Haig also gave Ford a list of options on how to handle Watergate when he became president, one of which was to pardon Nixon.

Haig and Ford both later denied that they had made a deal to pardon Nixon. However, Ford must have at least been considering a pardon from the time he became president. When Ford was asked on August 28 at his first press conference as president about a possible pardon, he replied, "It is an option and a proper option for any president."[87] Only 11 days later, on September 8, Ford announced that he was pardoning the former president.

In a televised speech, Ford told Americans that he felt sympathy for Nixon because of the disgrace and humiliation he and his family had already suffered. However, Ford said he was not pardoning Nixon because he felt sorry for him. Ford believed that legal proceedings against Nixon would further inflame the divisiveness and bitterness Watergate had created. He said, "My concern is the immediate future of this great country ... My conscience tells me clearly and certainly that I cannot prolong the bad dreams that continue to reopen a chapter that is closed. My conscience tells me that only I, as President, have the constitutional power to firmly shut and seal this book."[88]

The pardon covered any crimes Nixon committed as president. In accepting the pardon—an act many people believed proved he was guilty of the crimes that the House had charged him with—Nixon said, "No words can describe the depths of my regret and pain at the anguish which my mistakes over Watergate have caused the nation and the presidency."[89] Nixon admitted to having made mistakes, but many people were disappointed he did not admit he had done something illegal or morally wrong.

A 1974 Gallup poll showed that 53 percent of Americans opposed the pardon because they wanted Nixon to

President Ford's pardon of Nixon sharply divided the country. Ford's press secretary almost immediately resigned in protest, and the pardon likely cost Ford reelection in 1976.

stand trial. Many people also thought it was unfair for Nixon to be pardoned while others were still being tried and sentenced for Watergate crimes.

Nixon's Staff Sentenced

On March 1, 1974, the grand jury that had been considering Watergate charges since the burglary occurred indicted former U.S. attorney general John N. Mitchell and six White House aides—H. R. Haldeman, John Ehrlichman, Charles Colson, Gordon C. Strachan, Robert Mardian, and Kenneth Parkinson—for obstructing the investigation. The grand jury named Nixon as a coconspirator but did not charge him with any crimes. The "Watergate Seven" were tried by Sirica. On January 1, 1975, all but Parkinson were found guilty of various charges of obstructing the Watergate investigation and concealing Nixon's participation in the cover-up. Mardian was later cleared of all charges in a second trial.

When Mitchell was found guilty of

All the President's Men

Many people believe it was unfair that President Nixon escaped punishment for his involvement in Watergate while many of his aides were tried, convicted, and sent to prison. White House aides Haldeman, Ehrlichman, Colson, and Dean all went to prison along with other Watergate figures, including G. Gordon Liddy, who helped plan and carry out the burglary of the DNC offices. However, many of the central figures in Watergate benefited from the notoriety they gained from the political scandal after they were released from prison. Dean has written four books about his experiences. He was just one of many Watergate figures—including Haldeman, Liddy, and Judge John J. Sirica—who were paid to write books about their part in the historic event. Liddy served the longest sentence, nearly five years. When Liddy was released from prison, he capitalized on his Watergate fame and became a radio talk-show host and played small parts in movies and on television shows. Haldeman sold real estate and opened steak houses. He once said that instead of hurting him, his Watergate fame helped him in his business deals.

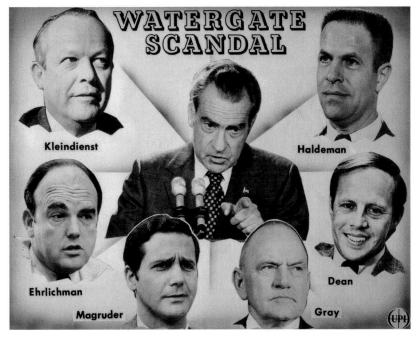

All administration officials who were involved in the Watergate scandal were forced to resign.

conspiracy, obstruction of justice, and perjury charges, he became the first former U.S. attorney general convicted of illegal activities and imprisoned. Sirica sentenced Mitchell to between two-and-a-half and eight years in prison; he only served nineteen months before being released because of poor health. Mitchell had been the one to approve G. Gordon Liddy's plan to bug the DNC offices. Afterward, Mitchell once angrily declared that when they met "I should have thrown Liddy out the window."[90]

Sirica was also the judge who tried and sentenced Liddy and the other men involved in the burglary—E. Howard Hunt, Bernard L. Barker, Virgilio R. Gonzalez, Eugenio R. Martinez, Frank A. Sturgis, and James W. McCord Jr. Before Sirica sentenced them on March 23, 1973, he said, "The crimes committed by these defendants can only be described as sordid, despicable, and thoroughly reprehensible."[91] Liddy received the stiffest sentence and served 52 months in prison. The others had shorter sentences, because their crimes were less serious or they cooperated with authorities. McCord, whose testimony helped investigators discover the truth about Watergate, was in prison only four months.

John Dean III and Jeb Magruder were among 30 individuals who pled guilty and were indicted or convicted of charges related to Watergate or other illegal 1972 campaign activities, such as burglarizing the office of Daniel Ellsberg's psychiatrist. Twenty-one corporations, including American Airlines, Goodyear, and Hertz, were also found guilty of giving illegal contributions to Nixon's campaign. Another casualty of Watergate was President Ford. Democrat Jimmy Carter defeated Ford in the 1976 presidential election, and it was believed that lingering public anger over Nixon's pardon contributed to Ford's loss.

Kissinger once summed up the scope of the Watergate damage saying, "In destroying himself, Nixon had wrecked the lives of almost all who had come into contact with him."[92] The irony of Watergate is that Nixon, the central figure in the worst political scandal in U.S. history, stayed out of prison. What he had to bear was the humiliation of his resignation.

Saving His Legacy

While many of Nixon's former aides were imprisoned, Nixon was living at his luxurious oceanfront estate in San Clemente, California. As a consequence of his involvement in Watergate, the state of New York took away his law license, and he never practiced law again. Unable to work as a lawyer, Nixon began writing books and giving speeches. Nixon's infamy from Watergate helped him get a $2.5 million advance for writing his memoirs, which sold 330,000 copies in the first 6 months it was on sale in 1978.

Nixon was so desperate for money that in 1977, he agreed to a series of

The "-Gate" Effect

The Watergate scandal has achieved a strange immortality by lending part of its name to other major political scandals. Journalists routinely attach the suffix "-gate" to disgraceful or criminal situations.

"Monicagate" was the relationship turned perjury scandal involving President Bill Clinton's affair with White House intern Monica Lewinsky. "Irangate" was a scandal in the 1980s that involved illegal activities by members of President Ronald Reagan's administration, who sold weapons to Iran and diverted the proceeds to anti-Communist Contra rebels in Nicaragua. "Whitewatergate" was a controversy involving President Bill Clinton and Hillary Clinton that accused the White House of blocking investigations of a failed guarantee and loan business that the Clintons had ties to.

"Katrinagate" refers to the federal government's failure in 2005 to adequately help victims of Hurricane Katrina. "Climategate" broke in 2009 when emails of climate scientists were released to the public, suggesting that some climate research data was manipulated to quiet global-warming critics. An investigation into Climategate revealed no evidence of scientific misconduct.

"Russiagate" refers to the political scandal surrounding the belief that Russia interfered in the 2016 presidential election between Donald Trump and Hillary Clinton. As of 2018, this scandal is still ongoing.

interviews with English television host David Frost. Nixon was paid $600,000 plus a share of the profits from the sale of the interviews to television stations around the world. Frost recalled years later that "[Nixon] was obsessed with money."[93] Frost said Nixon feared that he would become poor if people who went to jail because of Watergate sued him.

Frost interviewed Nixon for nearly 30 hours, and the most fascinating questions and answers concerned Watergate. The interviews were developed into four television episodes, each ninety minutes long. When they were broadcast in the United States, the first episode drew an audience of 45 million viewers as people tuned in to see if Nixon would admit he had done something illegal. Nixon did not directly say he was guilty of any crimes. However, Nixon came close to confessing to his wrongdoing when he admitted, "I did abuse the power I had as president" and "I said things that were not true."[94]

President Bill Clinton gave a eulogy at Nixon's funeral in 1994. He reminded everyone to look at Nixon's entire life and not just the mistakes he made.

When Frost asked him if he had personally tried to conceal Watergate, Nixon replied, "Under the circumstances, I would have to say that a reasonable person could call [it] a cover-up ... I let the American people down. And I have to carry that burden with me for the rest of my life. My political life is over."[95]

In the last 19 years of his life, Nixon did everything he could to rehabilitate his public image. In his memoirs, Nixon tried to downplay the importance of the burglary by comparing it to similar acts of political espionage that Democrats had committed. His greatest achievements were in foreign policy, and Nixon visited many foreign countries to remind people of what he had done. He also wrote several books about foreign affairs, which showed his understanding of such issues and garnered praise, even from people who disliked him for Watergate.

By the time Nixon died on April 22, 1994, he had acquired the status of elder statesman, and he advised presidents and other officials about foreign affairs. Many people, however, never forgave him for Watergate and the ugly political division it created in the nation. At Nixon's funeral, Kissinger quoted a line from a play by Shakespeare to sum up the division of opinion that existed about Nixon. Kissinger said, "He was a man, take him for all in all. I shall not look upon his like again."[96] Kissinger wanted people to consider everything Nixon had done in his life, the good things as well as the bad. For most people, however, Nixon's lasting legacy remains his connection to Watergate.

The Impact of Watergate

As chairman of the Senate Watergate Committee, Senator Sam Ervin was instrumental in uncovering the truth behind the burglary at the Watergate Hotel. On July 25, 1973, when Nixon refused for the first time to turn over White House tapes, Ervin was saddened about the political scandal that was growing larger every day. He said, "I think that the Watergate tragedy is the greatest tragedy this country has ever suffered."[97] However, by 1982, even Ervin had realized that there was a positive side to the nation's gravest political scandal. Ervin said the ability of Congress and the courts to control a president who was abusing the power of his office showed the strength of the nation's democratic system of government. He said, "It proves to me that we have the most viable government on the face of the earth. I don't think that kind of thing could happen in any country but ours ... and that's all the more reason why we should keep this country great."[98]

The triumph of government that Ervin saw in Watergate was that the nation was able to survive an attempt by its most powerful official to cover up a crime without having the country fall into civil war. He believed that civil war could happen in a nation where the system of government does not have effective counterbalances to the power of the nation's leader. In 2007, Bob Woodward also claimed Watergate had been beneficial for the United States. He said,

> Watergate was probably a good thing for the country; it was a good, sobering lesson. Accountability to the law applies to everyone. The problem with kings and prime ministers and presidents is that they think they are above it, and there is no accountability, and that they have some special rights, and privileges, and statuses.[99]

In 1973, the Washington Post won the Pulitzer Prize for Public Service for Bob Woodward and Carl Bernstein's reporting on Watergate. Their heroic work in helping to uncover the facts in Watergate inspired a generation of journalists to investigate such situations harder than ever before. In 1997, on the 25th anniversary of Watergate, historian Stephen Wayne of Georgetown University said that the news media was still being affected positively by the political scandal. In the past, reporters had sometimes failed to question the veracity of presidential statements because the office of president was so important. Wayne said that after Watergate, "the press no longer gives public officials the benefit of the doubt … they assume if [a person is not lying], he's not telling the whole truth."[100] Reporters now serve as watchdogs for the public, digging up evidence on any wrongdoing in government.

According to Haig, Nixon tarnished the image of the presidency forever. He said, "Nixon will always be remembered for it because the event had such major historic consequences for the country; a fundamental discrediting of respect for the presidency—the integrity of the office."[101]

"Here the People Rule"

Watergate can be looked at as the beginning of the end of American innocence in politics. Since Nixon's time as president, the division between Republicans and Democrats has grown deeper. Mistrust for government officials has become normal in America, and some political leaders try to capitalize on the mistrust to further their own interests. With the addition of social media dominating American culture and providing a platform for debate 24 hours a day, the chasm that divides public opinion continues to grow wider.

While one cannot unsee the corruption of the political system that Watergate revealed, one can learn from it. After the trial, laws were immediately passed requiring more careful disclosure of campaign finances. The public became more aggressive in demanding transparency from their government officials, and grassroots movements such as Occupy Wall Street, a movement that protested income inequality, prove that the public has not forgotten what can happen behind closed doors.

It is important, however, to recognize Watergate as a reflection of what is good about America. Watergate is an example that the democratic system of government works and that not even the president is above the laws of the United States. As Gerald Ford said in his first speech after Nixon's resignation, "Our Constitution works; our great Republic is a government of laws and not of men. Here the people rule."[102]

Notes

Introduction:
The End of American Innocence

1. Fred Emery, *Watergate: The Corruption of American Politics and the Fall of Richard Nixon*. New York, NY: Random House, 1994, p. xii.
2. Marc Fisher, "Watergate: The Long Shadow of a Scandal," *Washington Post*, June 14, 2012. www.washingtonpost.com/lifestyle/style/as-years-go-by-watergate-drifts-toward-myth/2014/06/14/cff4080c-aa8a-11e1-b15f-a61f-af9b4d76_story.html?utm_term=.acfa2d4e1a8d.

Chapter One:
"One of Us"

3. John Aloysius Farrell, "The Operatic Life of Richard Nixon," *The Atlantic*, January 9, 2013. www.theatlantic.com/politics/archive/2013/01/the-operatic-life-of-richard-nixon/266963.
4. Richard M. Nixon, *The Memoirs of Richard Nixon*. New York, NY: Grosset and Dunlap, 1978, p. 12.
5. Quoted in Mel Elfin and Gary Cohen, "Richard M. Nixon," *U.S. News & World Report*, May 2, 1994, p. 24.
6. Quoted in "LIFE Remembers Richard M. Nixon," *LIFE*, June 19, 1994, p. 16.
7. Quoted in Anthony Summers with Robbyn Swan, *The Arrogance of Power: The Secret World of Richard Nixon*. New York, NY: Penguin, 2001, p. 16.
8. Quoted in Robert Dallek, *Nixon and Kissinger: Partners in Power*. New York, NY: HarperCollins, 2007, p. 7.
9. Nixon, *The Memoirs of Richard Nixon*, p. 27.
10. Quoted in Summers, *The Arrogance of Power*, p. 45.
11. Quoted in Rick Perlstein, *Nixonland: The Rise of a President and the Fracturing of America*. New York, NY: Scribner, 2008, p. 31.
12. Karina Longworth, "Actress, Opera Star, Congresswoman," *Slate*, April 14, 2016. www.slate.com/articles/podcasts/you_must_remember_this/2016/04/you_must_remember_this_on_congresswoman_helen_gahagan_douglas_and_richard.html.
13. Quoted in Summers, *The Arrogance of Power*, p. 83.
14. Richard M. Nixon, "Checkers Speech," The History Place Great Speeches Collection, accessed on February 2, 2018. www.historyplace.com/speeches/nixon-checkers.htm.
15. Quoted in Nixon, *The Memoirs of Richard Nixon*, p. 181.

16. Quoted in Summers, *The Arrogance of Power*, p. 218.
17. Quoted in Perlstein, *Nixonland*, p. 61.
18. Quoted in David Greenberg, *Nixon's Shadow: The History of an Image*. New York, NY: Norton, 2003, p. 136.
19. Nixon, *The Memoirs of Richard Nixon*, p. 298.
20. Farrell, "The Operatic Life of Richard Nixon."

Chapter Two: A Third-Rate Burglary

21. H. R. Haldeman, *The Haldeman Diaries*. New York, NY: Berkley Books, 1995.
22. Carl Bernstein and Bob Woodward, "40 years After Watergate, Nixon was far Worse than we Thought," *Washington Post*, June 8, 2012. www.washingtonpost.com/opinions/woodward-and-bernstein-40-years-after-watergate-nixon-was-far-worse-than-we-thought/2012/06/08/gJQAlsi0NV_story.html?utm_term=.3e5c238a1a80.
23. Quoted in Summers, *The Arrogance of Power*, p. 332.
24. Quoted in Dallek, *Nixon and Kissinger*, p. 122.
25. Quoted in Emery, *Watergate*, p. 48.
26. Quoted in Richard Reeves, *President Nixon: Alone in the White House*. New York, NY: Simon & Schuster, 2001, p. 353.
27. Nixon, *The Memoirs of Richard Nixon*, pp. 451–452.
28. Quoted in Reeves, *President Nixon*, p. 213.
29. Quoted in Perlstein, *Nixonland*, p. 387.
30. Quoted in "The Plight of the Doves," *TIME*, September 14, 1970. www.time.com/time/magazine/article/0,9171,902748,00.html.
31. Quoted in Theodore H. White, *Breach of Faith: The Fall of Richard Nixon*. New York, NY: Atheneum, 1975, p. 158.
32. Quoted in Emery, *Watergate*, p. 118.
33. Quoted in G. Gordon Liddy, *Will*. New York, NY: St. Martin's, 1980, p. 325.
34. Emery, *Watergate*, pp. 134–135.
35. Quoted in "Intruders in Democratic Headquarters," *Washington Post*, June 14, 1992.

Chapter Three: Investigation and Cover-Up

36. Quoted in Dennis Byrne, "Are there Comparisons Between Nixon, Obama?," *Chicago Tribune*, May 28, 2013. www.chicagotribune.com/news/nationworld/politics/ct-oped-0528-byrne-20130528-column.html.
37. Quoted in Carl Bernstein and Bob Woodward, "The War on the News Media" in *All the President's Men*. New York, NY: Simon and Schuster, 1974, p. 18.
38. Lamar Waldron, *Watergate: The Hidden History: Nixon, the Mafia, and the CIA*. Berkeley, CA:

Counterpoint, 2012, p. 622.

39. Quoted in Emery, *Watergate*, p. 153.

40. Quoted in Bernstein and Woodward, *All the President's Men*, p. 18.

41. Quoted in Bernstein and Woodward, *All the President's Men*, p. 19.

42. Quoted in Perlstein, *Nixonland*, p. 678.

43. Quoted in Stanley I. Kutler, ed., *Abuse of Power: The New Nixon Tapes*. New York, NY: Simon & Schuster, 1997, p. 67.

44. Quoted in Bernstein and Woodward, *All the President's Men*, p. 25.

45. Quoted in Perlstein, *Nixonland*, p. 678.

46. Quoted in Greenberg, *Nixon's Shadow*, p. 190.

47. Quoted in Kutler, *Abuse of Power*, p. 54.

Chapter Four:
Taking Down a Presidency

48. Quoted in Emery, *Watergate*, p. 239.

49. John J. Sirica, *To Set the Record Straight: The Break-in, the Tapes, the Conspirators, the Pardon*. New York, NY: Norton, 1979, p. 88.

50. Quoted in Dallek, *Nixon and Kissinger*, p. 415.

51. Quoted in Reeves, *President Nixon*, p. 564.

52. Quoted in Gerald S. Strober and Deborah Hart Strober, *Nixon: An Oral History of His Presidency*. New York, NY: HarperCollins, 1994, p. 430.

53. Quoted in Bob Woodward, *Secret*

Man: The Story of Watergate's Deep Throat. New York, NY: Simon & Schuster, 2005, p. 93.

54. Quoted in Sirica, *To Set the Record Straight*, p. 96.

55. Quoted in Emery, *Watergate*, p. 269.

56. Quoted in Kutler, *Abuse of Power*, p. 247.

57. Quoted in Summers, *The Arrogance of Power*, p. 444.

58. Quoted in Liddy, *Will*, p. 278.

59. John Dean, *Blind Ambition: The White House Years*. New York, NY: Simon & Schuster, 1976, p. 218.

60. Richard Nixon, "President Richard Nixon First Watergate Speech, April 30, 1973 (The 'Saturday Night Massacre')," Virtual Library, accessed February 6, 2018. www.vlib.us/amdocs/texts/nixon041973.html.

61. Carl Bernstein and Bob Woodward. "Dean Alleges Nixon Knew of Cover Up Plan," *Washington Post*, June 3, 1973. www.washingtonpost.com/wp-srv/national/longterm/watergate/articles/060373-1.htm.

Chapter Five:
The Nixon Tapes

62. Lawrence Meyer. "President Taped Talks, Phone Calls; Lawyer Ties Ehrlichman to Payments," *Washington Post*, July 17, 1973. www.washingtonpost.com/wp-srv/national/longterm/watergate/articles/071773-1.htm.

63. Quoted in James R. Dickenson, "Sen.

Sam Ervin, Key Figure In Watergate Probe, Dies," *Washington Post*, April 24, 1985. www.washingtonpost.com/wp-srv/national/longterm/watergate/stories/ervinobit.htm.

64. Quoted in George Lardner Jr., "Cox Is Chosen as Special Prosecutor, Democrat Served Under Kennedy as Solicitor General," *Washington Post*, May 19, 1973. www.washingtonpost.com/wp-srv/national/longterm/watergate/articles/051973-1.htm.

65. Quoted in Jules Witcover, "The First Day of Watergate: Not Exactly High Drama," *Washington Post*, May 18, 1973. www.washingtonpost.com/politics/the-first-day-of-watergate-not-exactly-high-drama/2012/06/04/gJQAsqjDJV_story.html?utm_term=.ab7a0eae7c3f.

66. Quoted in Donald Farinacci, *When One Stood Alone: John J. Sirica's Battle Against the Watergate Conspiracy*. Bloomington, IN: AuthorHouse, 2009, p. 78.

67. Quoted in Peter Grier, "Howard Baker: The Real Story of His Famous Watergate Question," *Christian Science Monitor*, June 26, 2014. www.csmonitor.com/USA/Politics/Decoder/2014/0626/Howard-Baker-the-real-story-of-his-famous-Watergate-question.

68. Quoted in Mike Feinsilber, "Expletives Deleted or Not, Secret Tapes Proved Fatal to Nixon Presidency," *Los Angeles Times*, June 8, 1997. articles.latimes.com/1997-06-08/news/mn-1347_1_richard-nixon.

69. Quoted in Susanna McBee, "Court Battle Set as Nixon Defies Subpoenas," *Washington Post*, July 27, 1973. www.washingtonpost.com/wp-srv/national/longterm/watergate/articles/072773-1.htm.

70. Quoted in Reeves, *President Nixon*, p. 605.

71. Quoted in Conrad Black, *Richard M. Nixon: A Life in Full*. New York, NY: Public Affairs, 2007, p. 937.

72. Quoted in Carroll Kilpatrick, "Nixon Tells Editors, 'I'm Not a Crook,'" *Washington Post*, November 18, 1973. www.washingtonpost.com/politics/nixon-tells-editors-im-not-a-crook/2012/06/04/gJQA1RK6IV_story.html?utm_term=.1d72e-2b2ee57.

73. Quoted in Louis W. Liebovich, *Richard Nixon, Watergate, and the Press*. Westport, CT: Praeger, 2003, p. 102.

74. Nixon, *The Memoirs of Richard Nixon*, p. 993.

75. Barbara Charline Jordan, "Statement on the Articles of Impeachment," American Rhetoric, accessed on February 6, 2018. www.americanrhetoric.com/speeches/barbarajordanjudiciary statement.htm.

76. Quoted in Bob Woodward and Carl Bernstein, *The Final Days*. New York, NY: Simon & Schuster Paperbacks, 1976, p. 283.

77. Quoted in Woodward and Bernstein, *The Final Days*, p. 415.

78. Quoted in Emery, *Watergate*, p. 470.

79. Nixon, *The Memoirs of Richard Nixon*, p. 1078.

80. Richard M. Nixon, "President Nixon's Resignation Speech," PBS, August 8, 1974. www.pbs.org/newshour/spc/character/links/nixon_speech.html.

Epilogue:
The Watergate Effect

81. U.S. News Staff, "Effects of Watergate: The Good and the Bad," *U.S. News & World Report*, August 26, 1974. www.usnews.com/news/articles/2014/08/08/effects-of-watergate-the-good-and-the-bad.

82. Fisher, "The Long Shadow of a Scandal."

83. Gerald R. Ford, "Gerald R. Ford's Remarks on Taking the Oath of Office as President," Gerald R. Ford Library and Museum, August 9, 1974. www.fordlibrarymuseum.gov/library/speeches/740001.asp.

84. Ford, "Gerald R. Ford's Remarks on Taking the Oath of Office as President."

85. Quoted in Leon Jaworski, *The Right and the Power: The Prosecution of Watergate*. New York, NY: Reader's Digest Press, 1976, p. 227.

86. Quoted in Elizabeth Drew, *Richard M. Nixon*. New York, NY: Times Books, 2007, p. 134.

87. Quoted in Berry Werth, "The Pardon," *Smithsonian*, February 2007, p. 56.

88. Gerald Ford, "President Gerald Ford's Pardon of Richard Nixon," CNN, September 8, 1974. www.cnn.com/ALLPOLITICS/1997/gen/resources/watergate/ford.speech.html.

89. Quoted in White, *Breach of Faith*, p. 343.

90. Quoted in Emery, *Watergate*, p. 180.

91. Sirica, *To Set the Record Straight*, p. 118.

92. Quoted in Stephen E. Ambrose, *Nixon: Ruin and Recovery 1973–1990*. New York, NY: Simon & Schuster, 1992, p. 405.

93. Quoted in David Segal, "Interview with the Interviewer 'Frost/Nixon' Puts David Frost Back in the Public Eye," *Washington Post*, April 30, 2007.

94. Quoted in Drew, *Richard M. Nixon*, p. 138.

95. Quoted in "I Have Impeached Myself," *The Guardian*, September 7, 2007. www.theguardian.com/theguardian/2007/sep/07/greatinterviews1.

96. Quoted in David Von Drehle, "Richard Nixon's Long Journey Ends," *Washington Post*, April 27, 1994. www.washingtonpost.com/wp-dyn/articles/A99301-1994Apr28.html.

97. Quoted in Carroll Kilpatrick, "President Refuses to Turn Over Tapes; Ervin Committee, Cox Issue Subpoenas: Action Sets Stage for Court Battle on Powers Issue," *Washington Post*, July 24, 1973. www.washingtonpost.com/wp-srv/national/longterm/watergate/articles/072473-1.htm.

98. Quoted in Charles E. Claffey, "Sam Ervin; Nixon Still Owes Public a Confession," *Boston Globe*, June 17, 1982.

99. Quoted in Strober and Strober, *Nixon*, p. 505.

100. Quoted in Brooks Jackson, "A Watergate Legacy: More Public Skepticism, Ambivalence," CNN, June 12, 1997. www.cnn.com/ALL-POLITICS/1997/gen/resources/watergate/watergate.jackson/index.alt.html.

101. Quoted in Strober and Strober, *Nixon*, p. 529.

102. Quoted in Fisher, "The Long Shadow of a Scandal."

For More Information

Books

Archer, Jules. *Watergate: A Story of Richard Nixon and the Shocking 1972 Scandal*. New York, NY: Sky Pony Press, 2015.
Originally published in 1975, the updated version of this book tells the entire Watergate story with historic photos.

Felt, Mark, and John O'Connor. *Mark Felt: The Man Who Brought Down the White House*. New York, NY: Hachette Book Group, 2017.
This book is the story of Deep Throat told by the man himself.

Olson, Keith W. *Watergate: The Presidential Scandal That Shook America*. Lawrence, KS: University Press of Kansas, 2003.
Olson's book discusses how Watergate was shaped by the world events that were happening at the time.

Woodward, Bob, and Carl Bernstein. *All The President's Men*. New York, NY: Simon and Schuster, 1974.
All the President's Men is written by the influential journalists whose investigation exposed the Watergate scandal. This book tells the behind-the-scenes story of how the *Washington Post* brought down a president.

Websites

The Miller Center: Richard Nixon

millercenter.org/president/nixon
This website by the University of Virginia provides an overview of Nixon's life and insights on events happening at the time of Watergate, such as the Vietnam War.

The Nixon Library

www.nixonlibrary.gov/index.php
The website of the Nixon Library has information about Nixon, a timeline, and links to his secret recordings.

Washington Post: Watergate

www.washingtonpost.com/politics/watergate/
The *Washington Post* website has the original articles published at the time of the scandal and follow-up articles about where the people involved in Watergate are today.

Watergate and the Constitution

www.archives.gov/education/lessons/watergate-constitution
This National Archives website contains official information on Watergate, including documents and a detailed timeline of the events surrounding the scandal.

Index

A

Agnew, Spiro T., 56, 60
All the President's Men (Woodward and Bernstein), 54
American Airlines, 86
Arab-Israeli War, 60

B

Baker, Howard H., 68, 71
Baldwin, Alfred, 42, 47
Barker, Bernard L., 9, 42, 44, 47, 53, 57–58, 86
Barrett, John, 44
Bay of Pigs, 49, 51–52
Belsen, James A., 49
Bernstein, Carl, 10, 46, 49–50, 52, 54, 61, 80, 90
blackmail, 29, 75
Bork, Robert, 73
Brown, Pat, 26
Butler, Caldwell, 76
Butterfield, Alexander, 7, 68, 71

C

Cabinet Room, 7, 68
Cambodia, 30, 32, 37–38
Central Intelligence Agency (CIA), 42, 47, 49–50, 52, 80–81
Chambers, Whittaker, 19
"Checkers" speech, 6, 21
Church Committee, 80
Clawson, Ken W., 52
Clinton, Bill, 70, 87–88

Clinton, Hillary, 81, 87
Cold War, 16, 30
Colson, Charles, 52, 63, 84–85
Committee to Re-elect the President (CRP), 9–10, 40–42, 46–47, 50, 52–53, 63
Cox, Archibald, 70–73

D

Dean, John, III, 7, 50, 62–68, 71, 75, 85–86
Democratic National Committee (DNC), 8–9, 40–42, 44, 53–54, 85–86
Douglas, Helen Gahagan, 19
Duke Law School, 16

E

Ehrlichman, John, 34, 65–66, 71, 84–85
Eisenhower, Dwight D., 20–21, 23–24, 26
Ellsberg, Daniel, 29, 34, 41, 71, 86
Emery, Fred, 10, 44
Ervin, Sam J., 31, 68–70, 72, 89

F

Federal Bureau of Investigation (FBI), 10, 16, 32, 34, 50, 52, 61, 63, 66, 80
Felt, William Mark, Sr. ("Deep Throat"), 61, 63
Ford, Gerald R., 11, 60, 78–79, 82–84, 86, 91

Frost, David, 87, 89

G
Gallup poll, 32, 83
"-gate" suffix, 87
Goldwater, Barry, 26, 56, 78–79
Gonzalez, Virgilio R., 9, 42, 44, 47–48, 57–58, 86
Goodyear, 86
Gray, L. Patrick, 50, 52, 63
Gurney, Edward J., 68

H
Haldeman Diaries, The (Haldeman), 29
Haldeman, H. R., 7, 29, 50, 52, 55, 63–67, 73, 78, 84–85
Hatfield, Mark, 38
Hertz, 86
Hiss, Alger, 6, 19–20
House Judiciary Committee, 11, 73, 75, 82
House of Representatives, 70, 77, 82
House Un-American Activities Committee (HUAC), 6, 19
Humphrey, Hubert H., 28
Hunt, E. Howard, Jr., 10, 34, 41–44, 47, 50, 52–53, 57–58, 86

I
impeachment, 7–8, 11, 60, 70, 73, 75–79, 82
Inouye, Daniel K., 68

J
Jaworski, Leon, 73, 75, 82–83
Johnson, Andrew, 70
Johnson, Lyndon B., 26–29, 31, 33, 56
Jordan, Barbara, 76

K
Kennedy, John F., 6, 24–26, 48, 51, 82
Kent State University, 30, 36–38
Khrushchev, Nikita, 24
Kissinger, Henry, 46, 58, 61, 86, 89
Kitchen Debate, 24
Kleindienst, Richard, 47, 66, 70

L
LaRue, Frederick C., 42, 47
Leeper, Paul, 44
Liddy, G. Gordon, 10, 34, 40–44, 47, 57–58, 63–64, 85–86

M
Magruder, Jeb, 10, 42, 44, 46–47, 49–50, 86
Mardian, Robert, 84
Martinez, Eugenio R., 9, 42, 44, 47, 57–58, 86
McCord, James W., Jr., 9–10, 42, 44, 47, 49–50, 52, 57–58, 61–63, 65, 86
McGovern, George S., 8–9, 38–42, 54–56, 58
Mitchell, John, 10, 34, 40, 42, 47, 50, 62–63, 84, 86
Montoya, Joseph M., 68
Mueller, Robert, 81

N
National Security Agency (NSA), 80–81
New York Times, 32, 34

O

O'Brien, Lawrence, 42, 44, 53–55
Operation Gemstone, 40–41, 47, 50

P

paranoia, 12–13, 68
Parkinson, Kenneth, 84
Pearl Harbor, 16
Pentagon Papers, 29, 32–34

R

Rhodes, John, 78–79
Richardson, Elliot L., 70, 72–73, 80
Ruckelshaus, William, 73

S

Saturday Night Massacre, 73
Scott, Hugh, 78–79
Senate Select Committee on Presidential Campaign Activities, 68
Senate Watergate Committee, 10, 31, 68, 72, 75–76, 89
Shoffler, Carl, 44
Silbert, Earl, 52
Sirica, John, 57–58, 62–63, 65, 72, 75, 84–86
"smoking gun," 71, 78
Soviet Union, 12, 19–20, 42
Stennis, John C., 72
Strachan, Gordon C., 84
Sturgis, Frank A., 9, 42, 44, 47, 49, 57–58, 86
subpoenas, 7, 72–73, 76

T

tape recordings, 10, 68–69
transcripts, 7, 10, 73, 75
Trump, Donald, 81, 87

V

Vietnamization, 36–37, 58
Vietnam War, 6, 10, 26, 30, 32, 36, 38, 55–56, 59–60, 69
Voorhis, Jerry, 6, 16, 18–19

W

Walters, Vernon, 50, 52
Washington Post, 10, 46, 49–50, 52, 54, 61, 67, 90
"Watergate Seven," 84
Watergate: The Corruption of American Politics and the Fall of Richard Nixon (Emery), 10, 44
Weicker, Lowell P., 69
White House Special Investigations Unit (Plumbers), 34, 41
Wills, Frank, 44–45
Woods, Rose Mary, 73
Woodward, Bob, 10, 46, 49–50, 52, 54, 61, 80, 90
World War II, 16, 20, 25, 30

Z

Ziegler, Ron, 46, 79

Picture Credits

Cover Bruce Roberts/Science Source/Getty Images; pp. 4–5, 7 (top right), 14, 17, 20, 27, 36–37, 39, 56, 59, 62, 66, 85 Bettmann/Bettmann/Getty Images; pp. 6 (top), 43, 53, 75 Courtesy of the National Archives Catalog; p. 6 (bottom) William Bond/Keystone/Getty Images; p. 7 (top left) Arthur Schatz/The LIFE Picture Collection/Getty Images; p. 7 (bottom) Time Life Pictures/White House/The LIFE Picture Collection/Getty Images; p. 9 Frontpage/Shutterstock.com; p. 15 Courtesy of the Library of Congress; p. 18 David J. & Janice L. Frent/Corbis via Getty Images; pp. 22–23 Paul Schutzer/The LIFE Picture Collection/Getty Images; p. 25 Hulton Archive/Getty Images; p. 31 Keystone-France/Gamma-Keystone via Getty Images; p. 33 Robert Daemmrich Photography Inc/Corbis via Getty Images; p. 35 Universal History Archive/UIG via Getty Images; p. 41 Dan Godfrey/NY Daily News Archive via Getty Images; p. 48 AP Photo/Washington Metropolitan Police; p. 51 Three Lions/Getty Images; p. 61 Smith Collection/Gado/Getty Images; p. 69 Bdcousineau/Wikimedia Commons; p. 74 David Hume Kennerly/Getty Images; p. 78 Keystone/Hulton Archive/Getty Images; p. 81 The Guardian via Getty Images; p. 84 Courtesy Gerald R. Ford Library; p. 88 J. DAVID AKE/AFP/Getty Images.

About the Author

Christine Honders has written more than 20 books for young people on subjects including politics, American history, and economics. She lives in upstate New York with her husband and three children.